Family Tree Pocket Reference

family tree Pocket Reference

From the Editors of *Family Tree Magazine*

FAMILY
TREE
BOOKS

Cincinnati, Ohio
shopfamilytree.com

FAMILY TREE POCKET REFERENCE. Copyright ©2010 by the editors of *Family Tree Magazine*. Manufactured in the United States of America. All rights reserved. No other part of this book may be reproduced in any form or by any electronic or mechanical means including information storage and retrieval systems without permission in writing from the publisher, except by a reviewer, who may quote brief passages in a review. Published by Family Tree Books, an imprint of F+W Media, Inc., 4700 East Galbraith Road, Cincinnati, Ohio 45236. (800) 289-0963. First edition.

For more genealogy resources, visit <**shopfamilytree.com**>.

14 13 12 11 10   5 4 3 2 1

Distributed in Canada by Fraser Direct
100 Armstrong Ave.
Georgetown, Ontario, Canada L7G 5S4
Tel: (905) 877-4411

**Distributed in the U.K. and Europe
by David & Charles**
Brunel House, Newton Abbot, Devon,
TQ12 4PU, England
Tel: (+44) 1626-323200,
Fax: (+44) 1626-323319
E-mail: postmaster@davidandcharles.co.uk

Distributed in Australia by Capricorn Link
P.O. Box 704, Windsor, NSW 2756 Australia
Tel: (02) 4577-3555

Library of Congress Cataloging-in-Publication Data available from the publisher upon request.

*fw
media*

EDITED BY
Diane Haddad

DESIGNED BY
Christy Miller

PRODUCTION
COORDINATED BY
Mark Griffin

TABLE OF Contents

Introduction

Y ou're knee deep in genealogy research at your local library when you come across a strange term. You're in a court records class and the instructor throws out an unfamiliar acronym. You're searching the census on Ancestry.com when you realize you need the census date to calculate your great-grandfather's age.

You could stop what you're doing and search for the right book or website to get the definition or date you need. Or you could pull out your handy *Family Tree Pocket Reference*, look up what you need to know and get on with your research.

We've gathered key resource lists, definitions, dates and other reference information from *Family Tree Magazine* and FamilyTreeMagazine.com **<familytreemagazine. com>** and put it all into this handy pocket-size guide. Keep it in your library tote bag, your top desk drawer or, yes, your pocket, and use as needed.

How to Use This Book

Check the table of contents of this book to familiarize yourself with the information inside it. When you come across a genealogy word or acronym you don't know, need a statehood date, want to try a new website, wonder about the origin of a surname, have to calculate a Soundex code, need to know whether a family tree program is available for a Mac, want to learn how common your national heritage is, or need other pertinent information, just check the table of contents of this book, turn to the appropriate chapter and go to the section you need. Whenever your research uncovers a new resource or information that's pertinent to your family history, write it down in chapter 15, designed especially for you to record your favorite reference material.

RESEARCH BASICS

{A}

ABSTRACT: An abbreviated transcription of a document that includes the date of the record and every name in it; it may also provide relationships of the people mentioned.

ADMIXTURE: Ancestry that originates from more than one ethnic group.

AHNENTAFEL: German for "ancestor table," this system of pedigree chart numbering gives each ancestor a number. Fathers are even numbers; mothers, odd. Double the child's number to get the father's (if you're 1, your father is 2). Add one to the father's number to get the mother's (your mother is 3).

ALIQUOT PARTS: In the rectangular survey system, a description for a subdivision of a section of land using directions and fractions to indicate the land's location: W½ SE¼ represents the west half of the southeast quarter of a township.

ALLELE RESULT: Also called a marker value, the numeric value assigned to a genetic marker.

ANCESTORS: Relatives you descend from directly, including parents, grandparents, great-grandparents and so on.

AUTOSOMAL DNA: Genetic material inherited equally from mother and father (all your DNA except what's on the X and Y chromosomes); it's less useful genealogically than Y-DNA and mtDNA because it mutates more often. Genetic tests to determine ethnic origins typically analyze autosomal DNA.

{B}

BANNS (OR MARRIAGE BANNS): Church documents publicly stating couples' intent to marry.

BLOCK NUMBER: A one-, two-, or three-digit number that describes a block (or piece) of land within a township.

BOND: A written, signed and witnessed agreement requiring someone to pay a specified amount of money by a given date.

BOUNTY LAND: Land granted by the Colonial and federal governments as a reward for military service; bounty-land warrants—documents granting the right to the land—were assigned to soldiers, their heirs or other individuals.

BUREAU OF LAND MANAGEMENT GENERAL LAND OFFICE (GLO): The US government office historically in charge of dispersing public land. Usually, several branch land offices existed for each state; its website **<www.glorecords.blm.gov>** has a database with digitized federal land patents.

{C}

CEMETERY RECORDS: Records of those buried, as well as maps of grave sites; usually kept by cemetery caretakers.

CENSUS: An official count of the population in a given area; other details, such as names, ages, citizenship status and ethnic background of individuals, may be recorded. The US government has been collecting census data every 10 years since in 1790. Selected states have conducted their own censuses as well.

CERTIFIED COPY: A record copy made and attested to by custodians of the original who are authorized to give copies.

CHROMOSOME: A threadlike strand of DNA that carries genes and transmits hereditary information.

CLUSTER GENEALOGY: Studying your ancestor as part of a group of relatives, friends, neighbors, coworkers and associates; this approach can help you learn details you might miss by looking only at records of an individual ancestor.

COLLATERAL RELATIVE: Any kin who aren't in your direct line, such as siblings, aunts, uncles and cousins.

CONFIDENCE RANGE OR CONFIDENCE INTERVAL: A DNA results report shows the most likely ancestry percentages (for a bio-geographic test) or date an MRCA lived (for a Y-DNA test), as well as a confidence range showing other possible results.

CREDIT PATENT: A document transferring land to be paid for in installments over a four-year period. A delinquent payment or nonpayment of the full balance resulted in forfeiture. In 1820, Congress required payment for land at the time of the purchase.

{D}

DECLARATION OF INTENTION: An alien's sworn statement that he or she wants to become a US citizen, also called "first papers"; these court records list details such as name, age, occupation, birthplace, last foreign residence and more.

DEED: A document transferring ownership and title of property; unlike a patent, a deed records the sale of property from one private individual to another.

DESCENDANT CHART: A report displaying names and information on a person's descendants.

DESCENDANTS: An ancestor's offspring—children, grandchildren and every new generation in the direct line.

DNA: The molecule that contains each cell's genetic code, organized into 23 pairs of chromosomes; genetic genealogy tests analyze your Y-DNA, mtDNA or autosomal DNA.

DOCUMENTATION: The process of citing sources of the family history information you've gathered, making it easier to keep track of the research you've completed and allowing others to verify your findings.

{E}

ENUMERATION DISTRICTS: Divisions of each county and some large cities used to make census taking more efficient and accurate. For large cities, the boundaries of enumeration districts often match those of wards or precincts.

{F}

FAMILY GROUP RECORD (OR SHEET): A worksheet that succinctly summarizes your information on a couple and their children; includes names; dates and places of birth, baptism, marriage, death and burial; and source citations.

FAMILY HISTORY LIBRARY (FHL): The world's largest collection of genealogical information, founded in 1894 by the Church of Jesus Christ of Latter-day Saints (LDS church). The main branch is in Salt Lake City, Utah, but many of the library's microfilmed records can be rented for use at one of its worldwide Family History Centers. The FamilySearch website **<www.familysearch.org>** contains genealogical databases and the library's catalog.

FIVE-GENERATION ANCESTOR CHART: a family tree chart with five columns reading from left to right; they contain vital information for a person (in column 1) and his or her parents (column 2), grandparents (column 3) and so on.

FREEDMAN: A person released from slavery.

{G}

GAZETTEER: A geographical dictionary; a book giving names and descriptions of places, usually in alphabetical order.

GEDCOM: GEnealogy Data COMmunications, the universal file format for genealogy databases that allows users of different software programs to share their data with others.

GENE: A hereditary unit consisting of a sequence of DNA that occupies a specific location on a chromosome, and determines a particular characteristic in an organism.

GENEALOGY: The study of your family's history; the process of tracing your ancestors back through time.

GENETIC MARKER: Represents a specific location on a chromosome where the basic genetic units exist in a variable number of repeated copies.

GENOTYPE/SIGNATURE: The compilation of multiple genetic markers; the unique genetic identifier for any given individual.

{H}

HAPLOGROUP: An identification of the genetic group your ancient ancestors (10,000 to 60,000 years ago) belonged to, sometimes referred to as a branch of the world's family tree.

HAPLOTYPE: Collectively, the marker values on your Y-DNA test results.

HOMESTEAD: A home on land obtained from the US government; the homesteader agreed to live on the land and make improvements, such as adding buildings and clearing fields.

HOMESTEAD ACT OF 1862: A law allowing people to settle up to 160 acres of public land if they satisfied certain requirements; the land was free, but the settler paid a filing fee.

HVR (HYPERVARIABLE REGION): Sections of mtDNA (such as HV1 and HV2) used to determine your haplogroup.

{I}

INDEX: In genealogical terms, a list of names taken from a set of records. For example, a census index may list the names of people recorded in a given area in the 1870, 1880, 1900 or another census. Indexes come in book form as well as in searchable online databases, on CD, microfilm and microfiche. They usually provide source information for the source records.

INTERNATIONAL GENEALOGICAL INDEX (IGI): a pedigree database on the FamilySearch website; contains roughly 250 million names either submitted to the church or extracted from records the church has microfilmed.

INTESTATE: Describes a person who died without a will.

{J}

JULIAN CALENDAR: The calendar used from 46 BC to 1582, named for Julius Caesar; it's often referred to as the "Old Style" calendar and was replaced by the Gregorian calendar.

{K}

KINDRED: Blood relatives.

{L}

LAND CLAIM: A settler's application to receive public land.

LAND-ENTRY CASE FILE: A file created when a person claimed land under an act of Congress, such as the Homestead Act of 1862; the person first filled out an application at the local General Land Office. The file might contain marriage, immigration or other documents. Files are available from the National Archives and Records Administration.

LAND GRANT: Public land given to an individual by the government, usually as a reward for military service.

LAND PATENT: A document transferring land ownership from the federal government to an individual.

LEGACY: Property or money bequeathed to someone in a will.

LEGAL LAND DESCRIPTION: In a land patent, an exact identification of the land being transferred using survey terms.

LIEN: A claim placed on property by a person who is owed money.

LOCAL HISTORY: Usually, a book about the development of a town or county; these were popular in the late 19th century and often include details of the area's prominent families.

{M}

MANUSCRIPTS: Documents and records such as diaries, letters, family Bible entries and organizations' papers; you can find manuscript collections with the National Union Catalog of Manuscript Collections (NUCMC) search of library holdings.

MEDICAL RECORDS: Paperwork associated with medical treatments from hospitals, asylums, doctors or midwives; may be considered private documents and inaccessible to the public.

MERIDIAN: An imaginary north-south line; a principal meridian is the starting point for a rectangular land survey.

METES AND BOUNDS: A land survey method employing compass directions, landmarks and distances between points.

MILITARY RECORDS: Records of military service kept by the federal government (from the Revolutionary War to the present) and state government (for state militias and guards); examples are service records, pensions, bounty land warrant applications, draft registration cards and discharge papers.

MIRACODE SYSTEM: An indexing system similar to Soundex used to organize the results of the 1910 census; the computer-generated cards are organized first by Soundex code, then alphabetically by county, then alphabetically by given name.

MITOCHONDRIAL DNA: Genetic material mothers pass on to male and female children. Because it's passed down relatively unchanged, mtDNA can reveal "deep ancestry" along your maternal line—but not definitive links to recent generations.

MORTALITY SCHEDULE: A special federal census schedule listing persons who died during the census year.

MRCA (MOST RECENT COMMON ANCESTOR): The most recent ancestor two individuals descend from.

MUTATION: Changes in DNA that can reveal how long ago an MRCA lived when two people have similar marker values.

{N}

NATIONAL ARCHIVES AND RECORDS ADMINISTRATION (NARA): The United States' repository for federal records, including censuses, military service and pension records, passenger lists and bounty-land warrants; in addition to the primary archives in Washington, DC, NARA has a branch in College Park, Md., and 13 regional facilities across the nation.

NEW ENGLAND HISTORICAL AND GENEALOGICAL REGISTER SYSTEM: A genealogical numbering system showing an individual's descendants by generation. All children in a family get Roman numerals (i, ii, iii ...) and every child later listed as a parent also gets an Arabic numeral (2, 3, 4 ...). The system is named for the journal of the New England Historic Genealogical Society.

NGS QUARTERLY (NGSQ) SYSTEM: A narrative report showing an individual's descendants by generation. It uses an alternative numbering system to the Register report (above) in which every child in a family gets both a Roman numeral and an Arabic numeral. A plus sign indicates that a child appears as a parent in the next generation. The system is named for the journal of the National Genealogical Society.

{O}

ORAL HISTORY: A collection of family stories told by a family member or friend.

ORPHAN ASYLUM: An orphanage, or home for children whose parents have died.

{P}

PASSENGER LIST: Lists of names and information about passengers who arrived on ships into the United States; submitted to customs collectors at every port by the ship's master. Passenger lists weren't officially required by the US government until 1820.

PEDIGREE: List of a person's ancestors.

PENSION (MILITARY): A benefit paid regularly to a veteran (or his widow) for military service or a military service-related disability.

PERIODICAL SOURCE INDEX (PERSI): A print and online index to thousands of genealogy and local history periodicals published in the United States and Canada back to the 1700s; PERSI is a project of the Allen County Public Library in Fort Wayne, Ind., and available through HeritageQuest Online.

PLAT: A drawing showing the boundaries and features of a piece of property; in genealogy, creating such a drawing from a metes-and-bounds or legal land description as a surveyor would have done.

PETITION FOR NATURALIZATION: An alien resident's request to be made a citizen, often called "second papers" because it was submitted after filing a declaration of intention and fulfilling any residency requirements.

PRE-EMPTION: The right of a settler to acquire property that he had occupied before the government officially sold or surveyed it.

PRIMARY SOURCE: A record or other source created at the time of a particular event; a primary source is always the original record—birth and death certificates are primary sources for those events. An original record isn't always a primary source: A death certificate isn't a primary source of birth information.

PROBATE RECORDS: Records disposing of a deceased individual's property; they may include an individual's last will and testament. Information varies, but may include the name of the deceased, his age at death, property, family members and last place of residence.

PUBLIC LAND: Land originally owned by the federal government and sold to individuals.

{Q}
QUAKER: A member of the religious group called the Society of Friends; Quakers kept detailed records of their congregations, including vital statistics.

QUARTER SECTION: In the rectangular survey system, one-fourth of a section of land, equal to 160 acres.

{R}
RANGE: A row or column of townships lying east or west of the principal meridian and numbered successively to the east and to the west from the principal meridian.

REAL PROPERTY: Land and anything attached to it, such as houses, building, barns, growing timber and growing crops.

RECOMBINATION: The process by which chromosomes cross and switch genetic material at conception.

RECTANGULAR SURVEY SYSTEM: The land survey method the US General Land Office used most often; it employs base lines, one east-west and one north-south, that cross at a known geographic position. Townships—each generally 24 miles square—are described in relation to the base lines. Townships are subdivided into sections.

{S}

SECONDARY SOURCE: A record created after an event occurred, such as a biography, local history, index or oral history interview; original records can be secondary sources for information about earlier events (a death certificate is a secondary source for a birth date).

SECTION: A division of land within a township that measures one square mile (640 acres)—about 1/36 of a township; sections were further subdivided into half sections, quarter sections and sixteenth sections, or into lots.

SELF-ADDRESSED, STAMPED ENVELOPE (SASE): Include an SASE when you request records from people and institutions.

SNP (SINGLE NUCLEOTIDE POLYMORPHISM): Harmless mutations in autosomal DNA that can indicate where your ancient ancestors came from.

SOCIAL SECURITY DEATH INDEX: An index of Social Security Death records; includes names of deceased Social Security recipients whose relatives applied for Social Security Death Benefits after their passing.

SOUNDEX: A system of coding surnames based on how they sound, used to index the 1880 and later censuses; Soundex is useful in locating records containing alternate surname spellings. Soundex cards are arranged by Soundex code, then alphabetically by given name.

STATE LAND: Land originally owned by a state or another entity, rather than the federal government.

STR (SHORT TANDEM REPEAT): A type of DNA marker used to determine relationships between individuals.

{T}

TOWNSHIP: In a government survey, it's a square tract 6 miles on each side (36 square miles); a name given to the civil and political subdivisions of a county.

TRACT: A parcel of land that isn't fully contained within a single section; tracts within a township are numbered beginning with 37 to avoid confusion with section numbers.

{U}

UNION LIST OR CATALOG: A bibliography or catalog of materials held by multiple repositories, such as the National Union Catalog of Manuscript Collections, a finding aid for personal papers in institutions nationwide.

USURY: Historically, all interest paid.

{V}

VISITATION NUMBER: On a 1910 Miracode index card, the house number of the indexed individual.

VITAL RECORDS: Official records with basic information about a person's birth, marriage and/or divorce date and place, and death date and burial place.

VOLUME NUMBER: On a Soundex or Miracode index card, the number of the census volume with the indexed name.

VOTER REGISTRATION: A list of registered voters for each state; voter registration lists are sometimes the first public records of former slaves. Many states have microfilmed their lists or make them available on interlibrary loan.

{W}

WILL: A document in which a person outlines what should be done with his or her estate after death; the legal process to see that those instructions are carried out is called probate.

WITNESS: A person who sees an event and signs a document attesting to its content being accurate; family members, friends, neighbors and business associates commonly witnessed documents.

{X}

X: What the signer of a document would often write if he couldn't write his name; a witness would typically label this "his mark."

{Y}

Y CHROMOSOME: Genetic material passed down from father to son; because surnames also pass this way, Y-DNA tests can confirm (or disprove) genealogical links through a paternal line. Y-DNA surname studies are the most popular application of genetic genealogy.

Y-DNA: Genetic material fathers pass on to their sons.

{Z}

ZOUAVES: A name adopted by some Civil War Union volunteer regiments, who wore brightly colored uniforms, similar to the French light infantry units of the same name.

INSIDER'S GUIDE TO
GENEALOGY ACRONYMS

AAGG: African-American Genealogy Group

AAHGS: Afro-American Historical and Genealogical Society

ACPL: Allen County Public Library in Fort Wayne, Ind.

AGBI: American Genealogical-Biographical Index

AAD: Access to Archival Databases, part of the National Archives and Records Administration (NARA) website

AIC: American Institute for Conservation of Historic and Artistic Works

ALE: Ancestry Library Edition, a data service available through many public libraries

APG ("ap-jen"): Association of Professional Genealogists

ARC: Archival Research Catalog, part of NARA's website

BCG: Board for Certification of Genealogists

CG: Certified Genealogist

CGL: Certified Genealogical Lecturer

CMSR: Compiled Military Service Record

CWSS: Civil War Soldiers & Sailors System

DAR: Daughters of the American Revolution (also **NSDAR:** National Society Daughters of the American Revolution)

ED: Enumeration District, a geographical division defined for a US census

FEEFHS ("feefs"): Federation of East European Family History Societies

FGS: Federation of Genealogical Societies

FHC: Family History Center, a branch of the Family History Library

FHL: Family History Library in Salt Lake City

FHLC: FHL catalog

FOIA: Freedom of Information Act

FTDNA: Family Tree DNA, a genetic genealogy company

FTM: Family Tree Maker genealogy software

GAR: Grand Army of the Republic, a network of organizations for Civil War Union veterans

GEDCOM ("jed-com"): Genealogical Data Communications, the computer file format for family tree data (*.ged* is the extension for these files)

GENWISE: Genealogy Wise, a social networking website for genealogists

GLO: Bureau of Land Management General Land Office

GOONS: Guild of One-Name Studies

GPS: Genealogical Proof Standard

HQO: HeritageQuest Online genealogy databases, offered through many libraries

IAJGS: International Association of Jewish Genealogical Societies

ICAPGEN ("eye-cap-jen"): International Commission for the Accreditation of Professional Genealogists

IGI: International Genealogical Index, on the FamilySearch website

ISFHWE ("ish-wee"): International Society of Family History Writers and Editors

ISOGG: International Society of Genetic Genealogy

LOC: Library of Congress

MRCA: Most Recent Common Ancestor, the most recent ancestor you share with another person

MTDNA: Mitochondrial DNA

NARA ("nar-uh"): National Archives and Records Adminstration

NEHGS (sometimes called "hiss-jen"): New England Historic Genealogical Society, headquartered in Boston

NERGC: New England Regional Genealogy Conference

NGS: National Genealogical Society

NUCMC ("nuk-muk"): National Union Catalog of Manuscript Collections

OR: The Civil War reference *The War of the Rebellion: A Compilation of the Official Records of the Union and Confederate Armies*

PAF: Personal Ancestral File genealogy software

PALAM ("pal-am"): Palatines to America

PERSI ("per-zee"): Periodical Source Index to family history articles in US and Canadian magazines and journals

PRO: Public Record Office of the United Kingdom

RED BOOK: *Red Book: American State, County and Town Sources*

RM: RootsMagic genealogy software

SAR ("sar"): Sons of the American Revolution

SCGS: Southern California Genealogical Society

SCV: Sons of Confederate Veterans

SGGEE (sometimes pronounced "squeegee"): Society for German Genealogy in Eastern Europe

SMGF: Sorenson Molecular Genealogy Foundation

SUVCW: Sons of Union Veterans of the Civil War

TMG: The Master Genealogist genealogy software

UDC: United Daughters of the Confederacy

WDYTYA?: The genealogy television series "Who Do You Think You Are?" (can refer to NBC's US version or BBC's British version)

WRHS: Western Reserve Historical Society in Cleveland, Ohio

GENEALOGY ABBREVIATIONS

ABR. abridged; abridgement

ABT. about

ABS. or **ABST.** abstract

ACC. according to; account; accompanied

ADM. or **ADMIN.** administrator, administration

AKA or **ALS.** also known as; alias

AL alien

ANC. ancestor

APPX. appendix

B black (indicating race)

B. born

BP. or **BPT.** baptized; birthplace

BU. or **BUR.:** buried

CEM. cemetery

CH or **CH.** courthouse, children; church; chief; chaplain

CHR. christened

CIR., C. or **CA.** circa

CONF confirmed

CW Civil War

D. died

DECD. or **DEC'D.** deceased

DIV. divorced

DO or **DTO:** ditto

DOM. domestic

F female

FR family register

GDN. or **GRDN.** guardian

INF. infantry

INHAB inhabitant; inhabited

JUD. judicial

JUNR. junior

LIC. license

LIV. living

M. male or mulatto

M. or **MD.** married

MIL. military

MO. month

N negro

NA. naturalized

N.D. no date; not dated

NM never married

OBIT obituary

OS "Old Style" calendar

P.O.A. power of attorney

PR. proved; probated

P.R. parish register

RC Roman Catholic

REG. register

RES. residence; research

RET. retired

S. son

S. & H. son and heir

S/O: son of

SRNM. surname

T. or **TWP.** township

UNK. unknown

UNM. unmarried

W. widowed

COURT RECORDS LINGO

AFFIDAVIT: a statement of facts, signed under oath

BASTARDY BOND: the father of an "illegitimate" child agrees to pay support

ET AL.: Latin meaning "and others"

ET UX.: Latin meaning "and wife"

GUARDIAN: a person appointed by the court to manage property or protect the rights of another, such as a minor child

GUARDIAN AD LITEM: court-appointed person who represents someone incapable of managing his or her own affairs

INFANT: a person under the age of legal majority; often, 18 or 21

INSTANT or **INST.:** the same month as a previously stated date

INTERLINED: addition of words to a document, inserted between words or lines already written

ISSUE: children of a person

MOIETY: half of something

ORPHAN: a minor child who's lost one or both parents

SINE PROLE or **S.P.:** Latin meaning "without issue"

SURETY: one who agrees to be responsible for another, such as assuming financial responsibility for debts in case of default

FILLING OUT AN ANCESTOR CHART
AND FAMILY GROUP SHEET

1. Write surnames in capital letters. This lets you (or someone reading your charts) immediately distinguish last names from first and middle names. At first, this method might seem unnecessary—but when you run into kin with names such as Marian STACY or Guillaume GAUTIER de LACHENAYE, you'll see the importance.

2. If you know middle names, spell them out. This helps you distinguish Grandpa William Randolph Reynolds from Grandpa William Robert Reynolds. Remember, too, that some people went by their middle names, and that's how you'll often find them in records.

3. Record nicknames, denoting them in quotation marks. This is especially useful for kin whose nicknames don't relate to their real names, such as Everett "Butch" Smith.

4. List women's maiden names, not their married names. Since you're recording your female ancestors right next to their husbands, including their married names is redundant. If you don't know a woman's maiden name, note that with a question mark or simply skip the surname.

5. Format dates as day, month, full year. For consistency, genealogists record dates European-style, flip-flopping the American convention of month, day, year. To avoid confusion, use the month's abbreviation instead of a numeral. You know what 12 AUG 1836 means, whereas 12/8/1836 isn't so clear—is it Aug. 12 or Dec. 8? If you haven't yet established an exact date, use qualifiers such as *by 1836, before 1911* or *after 20 May 1893*. You can use abbreviations such as *c.* for circa, *abt.* for about, *bef.* for before, *aft.* for after and *bet.* for between

20 MUST-ASK ORAL HISTORY QUESTIONS

Ask open-ended questions (rather than ones with yes or no answers) during oral history interviews, and focus on people's experiences, not just names and dates. Start your question list with:

1. What's your first memory?

2. Who's the oldest relative you remember (and what do you remember about him or her)?

3. How did your parents meet?

4. Tell me about your childhood home.

5. How did your family celebrate holidays?

6. How did you meet your spouse?

7. Tell me about your wedding day.

8. Tell me about the day your first child was born.

9. What were your favorite school subjects?

10. Tell me about your favorite teacher.

11. Tell me about some of your friends.

12. Describe your first job.

13. What did you do with your first paycheck?

14. What was your favorite job and why?

15. Who are some of your heroes?

16. Where were you when you heard that President Kennedy had been shot? (Add or substitute other important historical events.)

17. What is your experience with or opinion of computers? (Add or substitute other modern conveniences, such as television, microwaves and cell phones.)

18. Tell me about some of your favorite songs (also books, movies and television shows).

19. Tell me about some of the places where you've been happiest.

20. What haven't we talked about that you'd like to discuss in the time we have left? (This is a good way to begin wrapping up the interview.)

SPOTTING ERRORS IN YOUR FAMILY TREE

Ask these questions to spot inaccurate names, dates and relationships in your family tree research:

1. Do all the dates make sense? Did someone accidentally type 1966 instead of 1866?

2. Does the chronology for each family group make sense? Is a mom giving birth too young or too old? Is a man marrying at age 12? Are children born at least nine months apart? Is a child being born after the mother is dead? Or is a child born before its parents?

3. When you find research showing a child in his parents' family group who was then carried forward as an adult, do the child's details (such as date and place of birth) match the adult information?

4. What sources did the compiler use? Did she consult original records, such as censuses, passenger lists and deeds? Or did she rely on secondary sources (citing, for example, "World Family Tree," "Aunt Susie's notes" or "Ted's GEDCOM file") that might regurgitate erroneous information?

5. Does biographical information seem exaggerated and too good to be true?

6. Are conclusions faulty? Has a compiler misinterpreted a document because she doesn't understand the legal terms for a particular time period? What information is the compiler basing a parent-child relationship on?

MAJOR US GENEALOGICAL SOCIETIES

**AFRO-AMERICAN HISTORICAL
AND GENEALOGICAL SOCIETY**
Box 73067, Washington, DC 20056, **<www.aahgs.org>**

ASSOCIATION OF PROFESSIONAL GENEALOGISTS
Box 350998, Westminster, CO 80035, **<www.apgen.org>**

**FEDERATION OF EAST EUROPEAN
FAMILY HISTORY SOCIETIES**
Box 510898, Salt Lake City, UT 84151, **<www.feefhs.org>**

FEDERATION OF GENEALOGICAL SOCIETIES
Box 200940, Austin, TX 78720, (888) 347-1500,
<www.fgs.org>

**INTERNATIONAL ASSOCIATION OF JEWISH
GENEALOGICAL SOCIETIES**
<www.iajgs.org>

NATIONAL GENEALOGICAL SOCIETY
3108 Columbia Pike, Suite 300, Arlington, VA 22204, (800)
473-0060, <www.ngsgenealogy.org>

**NATIONAL SOCIETY,
DAUGHTERS OF THE AMERICAN REVOLUTION**
1776 D St. NW, Washington, DC 20006, (202) 628-1776,
<www.dar.org>

**NATIONAL SOCIETY,
SONS OF THE AMERICAN REVOLUTION**
1000 S. Fourth St., Louisville, Kentucky 40203, (502) 589-
1776, <www.sar.org>

NEW ENGLAND HISTORIC GENEALOGICAL SOCIETY
99 Newbury St., Boston, MA 02116, (888) 296-3447,
<www.newenglandancestors.org>

---

10 GO-TO GENEALOGY RECORDS

You'll consult a variety of records and resource as you trace
your family tree. These 10 most-used types of records will
likely figure into your research.

1. **HOME SOURCES:** awards, certificates, Bibles, photos and
other family papers

2. **US CENSUS RECORDS:** taken every 10 years since 1790;
census records are opened for researchers 72 years after
the census was taken. (Almost all of the 1890 census was
destroyed.)

3. BIRTH RECORDS: Most states required counties to track births starting in the late 1800s and early 1900s; individual towns and counties may have kept records earlier. States often restrict the public's access to birth records older than 75 or 100 years.

4. MARRIAGE RECORDS: These records work similarly to birth records as far as when and where they were kept. Look for marriage licenses, too, as well as church records and newspaper announcements.

5. DEATH RECORDS: These records include not only official death certificates—maintained by the same entities as birth certificates, often with fewer privacy restrictions—but also obituaries and the Social Security Death Index (which lists deaths reported to the Social Security Administration, mostly after 1962).

6. SHIP PASSENGER LISTS: Starting in 1820, US-bound ships had to keep lists of their passengers.

7. WWI DRAFT CARDS: Virtually every man born from 1872 to 1900 and living in the United States in 1917 and 1918 had to fill out a WWI draft registration card.

8. CITY DIRECTORIES: Like modern phone books, these annual directories list the residents of towns, and some rural areas.

9. SS-5: If you find your ancestor's Social Security number in the Social Security Death Index, request his application, or SS-5, from the Social Security Administration.

10. CIVIL WAR GENERAL INDEX CARDS: The 6.3 million Union and Confederate soldier names on these cards are searchable on the free Civil War Soldiers and Sailors System **<www.itd.nps.gov/cwss/soldiers.cfm>**.

6 GENEALOGY MYTHS TO AVOID

1. YOU CAN BUY YOUR FAMILY CREST. Cups, wall hangings and other family crest doodads are available online. But "families" don't have crests—rather, individuals do. Coats of arms must be granted, and to claim the right to arms, you must prove descent through a male line of someone to whom arms were granted.

2. THE 1890 CENSUS BURNED TO A CRISP. Actually, it didn't—it was waterlogged and lay around until some unknown person authorized its disposal. But some parts survived and are on NARA microfilm and in online census collections.

3. YOUR WHOLE FAMILY HISTORY IS ONLINE. If only! You can get lots of records online, including censuses, passenger lists, military records, digitized books. But errors abound in online indexes, transcriptions and family trees, and repositories hold richly detailed, lesser-known records. At some point, you'll want or need to log off and go to the library.

4. YOUR ANCESTOR WAS A CHEROKEE PRINCESS or George Washington, or you're related to John Brown. Many families have legends about famous kin, and of course it could be true—but stories tend to get embellished and even made up over time, so research them before passing them on as truth. You may have Cherokee blood, but there weren't any Cherokee princesses. George Washington can't be an ancestor because he never had children (Martha did, from her first marriage). Also, not everyone with the same last name is related.

5. THE COURTHOUSE BURNED; ALL THE RECORDS ARE GONE. But records caught in courthouse fires weren't always completely destroyed. Sometimes records survived, or copies had been sent to another office, or the clerk asked citizens for copies of their records, or you can find the same information elsewhere.

6. YOUR ANCESTOR'S NAME WAS CHANGED AT ELLIS ISLAND.
Passenger lists were created at the port of departure, and the
ship's master would give them to immigration officials at the
arrival port. Ellis Island officials just checked the names on the
list; they didn't change any names. Many immigrants changed
their own names after arrival in an effort to sound more
"American." See **<www.genealogy.com/88_donna.html>** for
more information on immigrant name changes.

USING A RELATIONSHIP CHART

You know two people are related but you can't figure out how?
Use the relationship chart on the opposite page and follow
these steps:

1. Identify the most recent common ancestor of the two individuals with the unknown relationship.

2. Determine the most recent common ancestor's relationship
to each individual (for example, grandparent or great-great-
grandparent).

3. In the topmost row of the chart, find the common ancestor's
relationship to the first individual.

4. In the far-left column, find the common ancestor's relationship to the second individual.

5. Trace the row and the column from step 4 until they meet.
The square where they meet shows the relationship between
the two individuals.

THE MOST RECENT COMMON ANCESTOR IS PERSON 1'S ...

THE MOST RECENT COMMON ANCESTOR IS PERSON 2'S ...

	Parent	Grandparent	Great-grandparent	Great-great grandparent	3rd-great grandparent	4th-great grandparent	5th-great grandparent	6th-great grandparent
Parent	sibling	nephew or niece	grandnephew or -niece	great-grandnephew or -niece	great-great grandnephew or -niece	third-great grandnephew or -niece	fourth-great-grandnephew or -niece	fifth-great-grandnephew or -niece
Grandparent	nephew or niece	first cousins	first cousins once removed	first cousins twice removed	first cousins three times removed	first cousins four times removed	first cousins five times removed	first cousins six times removed
Great-grandparent	grandnephew or -niece	first cousins once removed	second cousins	second cousins once removed	second cousins twice removed	second cousins three times removed	second cousins four times removed	second cousins five times removed
Great-great grandparent	great-grandnephew or -niece	first cousins twice removed	second cousins once removed	third cousins	third cousins once removed	third cousins twice removed	third cousins three times removed	third cousins four times removed
3rd-great grandparent	great-great grandnephew or -niece	first cousins three times removed	second cousins twice removed	third cousins once removed	fourth cousins	fourth cousins once removed	fourth cousins twice removed	fourth cousins three times removed
4th-great grandparent	third-great grandnephew or -niece	first cousins four times removed	second cousins three times removed	third cousins twice removed	fourth cousins once removed	fifth cousins	fifth cousins once removed	fifth cousins twice removed
5th-great grandparent	fourth-great grandnephew or -niece	first cousins five times removed	second cousins four times removed	third cousins three times removed	fourth cousins twice removed	fifth cousins once removed	sixth cousins	sixth cousins once removed
6th-great grandparent	fifth-great grandnephew or -niece	first cousins six times removed	second cousins five times removed	third cousins four times removed	fourth cousins three times removed	fifth cousins twice removed	sixth cousins once removed	seventh cousins

SECRETARY, COURT HAND OR GOTHIC, 1600S: This is the most common script found in 17th-century materials, and it's reflected in the handwriting style of early English immigrants. You'll also see Mayflower Century script, which is a combination of the Secretary style with Italian and, by 1700, Roundhand script.

ITALIAN, 1400S TO 1700S: Also called italics; this style is characterized by rounded letter formations. Queen Elizabeth of England used cursive Italian script.

ROUNDHAND OR COPPERPLATE, 1700 TO LATE 1800S: This style became popular as copybooks—self-teaching handwriting manuals—began to be printed by copperplate engraving. It's recognizable by thin upstrokes and thicker downstrokes. The s is formed by a long flourish that's easily confused with a *p* or an *f*.

SPENCERIAN, 1865 TO 1890: Characterized by flourishes, Spencerian handwriting reflected the feminine pursuits of the Victorian period. Writing was a slow process because of all the loops and the number of times the writer lifted the pen.

PALMER, 1880 TO 1960S: Partially in reaction to the time-consuming Spencerian writing, Austin Palmer developed this method of plain, legible script more suited to the fast pace of business offices.

D'NEALIAN, 1965 TO PRESENT: Many children learning to write today are taught this style. See **<www.dnealian.com>** for more examples.

GENEALOGY RECORDS CHECKLIST

Use this records checklist to spark your searches for common and lesser-known ancestral records.

▷ **Business and Employment Records**
- apprentice and indenture records
- doctors' and midwives' journals
- insurance records
- merchants' account books
- professional licenses
- railroad, mining and factory records
- records of professional organizations and associations
- social security application (SS5)
- company newsletters
- government patents

▷ **Cemetery and Funeral Home Records**
- burial records
- grave-relocation records
- tombstone inscriptions

▷ **Censuses**
- agriculture schedules (1850 to 1880)
- American Indian (special censuses)
- Civil War veterans schedules (1890)
- defective, dependent and delinquent (DDD)
  schedules (1880)
- federal population schedules (1790 to 1930)
- manufacturing/industry schedules (1810, 1820,
  1850 to 1880)
- mortality schedules (1850 to 1880, 1885)
- school censuses
- slave schedules (1850, 1860)
- social statistics schedules (1850 to 1870, 1885)
- state/territorial and local censuses

▷ Church Records
- baptism and christening records
- confirmation records
- congregational histories
- marriage banns
- meeting minutes
- membership, admission and removal records
- ministers' journals

▷ Court Records
- adoption records
- bastardy cases
- civil records
- coroners' files
- criminal records
- custody papers
- estate inventories
- guardianship papers
- insanity/commitment orders
- licenses and permits
- marriage bonds, licenses and certificates
- military discharges
- minute books
- name changes
- naturalizations
- property foreclosures
- voter registrations
- wills
- wolf-scalp bounties

▷ Directories
- biographical
- city
- professional/occupational
- telephone

▷ Home Sources
- baptism and confirmation certificates
- birth certificates and baby books
- checkbooks and bank statements
- death records and prayer cards
- diaries and journals
- family Bibles
- funeral/memorial cards
- heirlooms and artifacts
- letters and postcards
- marriage certificates and wedding albums
- medical records
- photographs
- recipe books
- school report cards, yearbooks and scrapbooks
- wills

▷ Immigration Records
- alien registration cards
- citizenship papers (declaration of intention, certificate of naturalization)
- passenger lists
- passports and passport applications

▷ Institutional Records
- almshouse
- hospital
- orphanage
- police
- prison
- school
- work-farm
- fraternal associations

▷ Land and Property Records
- deeds

- grants and patents
- homestead records
- mortgages and leases
- plat maps
- surveys
- tax rolls
- warrants

▷ **Military Records**
- Colonial wars
- Revolutionary War and frontier conflicts (War of 1812, Indian wars and Mexican War)
- Civil War
- Spanish-American War
- World War I
- World War II
- Korean War
- Vietnam War
- draft records
- pension applications
- records of relocations and internment camps for Japanese-Americans, German-Americans and Italian-Americans during World War II

▷ **Newspapers**
- birth announcements
- classified advertisements
- engagement, marriage and anniversary announcements
- ethnic newspapers and immigrant ship notices
- family reunion announcements
- gossip and advice columns
- legal notices
- local news
- obituaries/death notices
- runaway notices (slaves, indentured servants, wives)
- unclaimed-mail notices

▷ **Published Sources**
• compiled genealogies
• genealogical periodicals
• local and county histories
• record abstracts and transcriptions

▷ **Vital Records**
• amended birth certificate
• birth certificate
• delayed birth certificate
• death certificate
• marriage license and certificate
• stillbirth certificate
• divorce/annulment decree

STATES

US STATE FAST FACTS

STATE	STATEHOOD	PUBLIC OR STATE LAND STATE	FIRST EXTANT US CENSUS	STATEWIDE VITAL RECORDS BEGIN		
				BIRTH	MARRIAGE	DEATH
AL Alabama	1819	Public	1830	1908	1936	1908
AK Alaska	1959	Public	1900	1913	1913	1913
AZ Arizona	1912	Public	1870	1909	1909	1909
AR Arkansas	1836	Public	1830	1914	1917	1914
CA California	1850	Public	1850	1905	1905	1905
CO Colorado	1876	Public	1860 (as four territories), 1870 (as Colorado Territory), 1880 (as a state)	1907	1907	1907
CT Connecticut	1788	State	1790	1897	1897	1897
DE★ Delaware	1787	State	1800	1861	1847	1881
FL Florida	1845	Public	1830	1899	1927	1899
GA Georgia	1788	State	1820	1919	1952	1919
HI Hawaii	1959	State	1900	1842	1842	1859
ID Idaho	1890	Public	1850 (as Oregon Territory)	1911	1947	1911

STATE	STATEHOOD	PUBLIC OR STATE LAND STATE	FIRST EXTANT US CENSUS	STATEWIDE VITAL RECORDS BEGIN		
				BIRTH	MARRIAGE	DEATH
IL Illinois	1818	Public	1820	1916	1962	1916
IN Indiana	1816	Public	1820	1907	1958	1899
IA Iowa	1846	Public	1850	1880	1880	1880
KS Kansas	1861	Public	1860	1911	1913	1911
KY Kentucky	1792	State	1810	1911	1958	1911
LA* Louisiana	1812	Public	1810	1914	none	1914
ME Maine	1820	State	1790	892	1892	1892
MD Maryland	1788	State	1790	1898	1950	1898
MA Massachusetts	1788	State	1790	1841	1841	1841
MI Michigan	1837	Public	1820	1867	1867	1867
MN Minnesota	1858	Public	1820 (in Michigan Territory)	1900	1958	1908
MS Mississippi	1817	Public	1820	1912	1926	1912
MO Missouri	1821	Public	1830	1910	1881	1910

STATE	STATEHOOD	PUBLIC OR STATE LAND STATE	FIRST EXTANT US CENSUS	STATEWIDE VITAL RECORDS BEGIN		
				BIRTH	MARRIAGE	DEATH
MT Montana	1889	Public	1870	1907	1943	1907
NE Nebraska	1867	Public	1860	1905	1909	1905
NV Nevada	1864	Public	1850	1911	1968	1911
NH New Hampshire	1788	State	1790	1901	1901	1901
NJ New Jersey	1787	State	1830 (Cumberland County only in 1800)	1848	1848	1848
NM New Mexico	1912	Public	1850	1920	1920	1920
NY New York	1788	State	1790	1880	1880	1880
NC North Carolina	1789	State	1790	1913	1962	1913
ND North Dakota	1889	Public	1900	1907	1925	1907
OH Ohio	1803	Public	1820 (Washington County only in 1810)	1908	1949	1908
OK Oklahoma	1907	Public	1860	1908	1908	1908
OR Oregon	1859	Public	1850	1903	1906	1903
PA Pennsylvania	1787	State	1798	1906	1885	1906

STATES

STATE	STATEHOOD	PUBLIC OR STATE LAND STATE	FIRST EXTANT US CENSUS	STATEWIDE VITAL RECORDS BEGIN		
				BIRTH	MARRIAGE	DEATH
RI Rhode Island	1790	State	1790	1853	1853	1853
SC South Carolina	1788	State	1790	1915	1950	1915
SD South Dakota	1889	Public	1900	1905	1905	1905
TN* Tennessee	1796	State	1830	1908	1945	1908
TX* Texas	1845	State	1850	1903	1966	1903
UT Utah	1896	Public	1850	1905	1887	1905
VT Vermont	1791	State	1790	1955	1955	1955
VA Virginia	1788	State	1810 (partial)	1912	1912	1912
WA Washington	1889	Public	1860	1907	1968	1907
WV West Virginia	1863	State	1870 (earlier censuses as part of Virginia)	1917	1964	1917
WI Wisconsin	1848	Public	1820	1907	1907	1907
WY Wyoming	1890	Public	1870	1909	1941	1909

*Delaware's statewide birth and death records stop in 1863 and resume in 1881. Louisiana birth records are kept in parish clerk offices. Tennessee has no statewide birth or death records for 1913. Texas was established as the Republic of Texas (not a territory) in 1836.

ALABAMA DEPARTMENT OF ARCHIVES AND HISTORY
Box 300100, Montgomery, AL 36130,
(334) 242-4435, **<www.archives.state.al.us>**

ALASKA STATE LIBRARY
Box 110571, Juneau, AK 99811,
(907) 465-2921, **<library.state.ak.us>**

ARIZONA STATE LIBRARY, ARCHIVES AND PUBLIC RECORDS
1901 W. Madison, Phoenix, AZ 85009,
(602) 926-3720, **<www.lib.az.us>**

ARKANSAS HISTORY COMMISSION
1 Capitol Mall, Little Rock, AR 72201,
(501) 682-6900, **<www.ark-ives.com>**

CALIFORNIA STATE ARCHIVES
1020 O St., Sacramento, CA 95814, (916) 653–2246, **<www. sos.ca.gov/archives>**

COLORADO STATE ARCHIVES
1313 Sherman St., Room 1B-20, Denver, CO 80203,
(303) 866-2358, **<www.colorado.gov/dpa/doit/archives>**

CONNECTICUT STATE LIBRARY/STATE ARCHIVES
231 Capitol Ave., Hartford, CT 06106,
(860) 757-6511, **<www.cslib.org/archives>**

DELAWARE STATE ARCHIVES
121 Duke of York St., Dover, DE 19901,
<archives.delaware.gov>

STATE ARCHIVES OF FLORIDA
R.A. Gray Building, 500 S. Bronough St.,

Tallahassee, FL 32399, (850) 245-6700,
<dlis.dos.state.fl.us/index_researchers.cfm>

GEORGIA ARCHIVES
5800 Jonesboro Road, Morrow, GA 30260,
(678) 364-3700, **<www.sos.ga.gov/archives>**

HAWAII STATE ARCHIVES
Kekāuluohi Building, 'Iolani Palace Grounds,
364 S. King St., Honolulu, HI 96813,
(808) 586-0329, **<hawaii.gov/dags/archives>**

IDAHO STATE HISTORICAL SOCIETY
Public Archives and Research Library,
2205 Old Penitentiary Road, Boise, ID 83712,
(208) 334-3356, **<www.idahohistory.net>**

ILLINOIS STATE ARCHIVES
Norton Building, Capitol Complex, Springfield, IL 62756,
(217) 782-4682, **<www.cyberdriveillinois.com/
departments/archives/archives.html>**

INDIANA STATE ARCHIVES
6440 E. 30th St., Indianapolis, IN 46219, (317) 591-5222,
<www.in.gov/icpr/2358.htm>

STATE HISTORICAL SOCIETY OF IOWA
<www.iowahistory.org/archives>
Des Moines: State of Iowa Historical Building,
600 E. Locust, Des Moines, IA, 50319, (515) 281-5111
Iowa City: State Historical Society of Iowa,
402 Iowa Ave., Iowa City, IA, 52240, (319) 335-3916

KANSAS STATE HISTORICAL SOCIETY
6425 SW Sixth Ave., Topeka, KS 66615,
(785) 271-8681, **<www.kshs.org>**

KENTUCKY DEPARTMENT FOR LIBRARIES AND ARCHIVES
Box 537, Frankfort, KY 40602,
(502) 564-8300 ext. 346, **<www.kdla.ky.gov>**

LOUISIANA
3851 Essen Lane, Baton Rouge, LA 70809, (225) 922-1208,
<sos.louisiana.gov/tabid/53/default.aspx>

MAINE STATE ARCHIVES
84 State House Station, Augusta, ME 04333,
(207) 287-5790, **<www.maine.gov/sos/arc>**

MARYLAND STATE ARCHIVES
350 Rowe Blvd., Annapolis, MD 21401,
(800) 235-4045, **<www.msa.md.gov>**

MASSACHUSETTS ARCHIVES
220 Morrissey Blvd., Boston, MA 02125,
(617) 727-2816, **<www.sec.state.ma.us/arc>**

ARCHIVES OF MICHIGAN
Box 30740, Lansing, MI 48909,
(517) 373-1408, **<www.michigan.gov/dnr/
0,1607,7-153-54463_19313---,00.html>**

MINNESOTA STATE ARCHIVES
345 W. Kellogg Blvd., St. Paul, MN 55102,
(651) 259-3300, **<www.mnhs.org/preserve/records>**

MISSISSIPPI DEPARTMENT OF ARCHIVES AND HISTORY
Box 571, Jackson, MS 39205,
(601) 576-6876, **<mdah.state.ms.us>**

MISSOURI STATE ARCHIVES
Box 1747, Jefferson City, MO 65102,
(573) 751-3280, **<www.sos.mo.gov/archives>**

MONTANA HISTORICAL SOCIETY
Box 201201, Helena, MT 59620,
(406) 444-2694, **<www.his.state.mt.us>**

NEBRASKA STATE HISTORICAL SOCIETY
Box 82554, 1500 R St., Lincoln, NE 68501,
(402) 471-3270, **<www.nebraskahistory.org>**

NEVADA STATE LIBRARY AND ARCHIVES
00 N. Stewart St., Carson City, NV 89701,
(775) 684-3360, **<nsla.nevadaculture.org>**

**NEW HAMPSHIRE DIVISION OF
ARCHIVES AND RECORDS MANAGEMENT**
71 S. Fruit St., Concord, NH 03301,
(603) 271-2236, **<www.sos.nh.gov/archives>**

NEW JERSEY STATE ARCHIVES
225 W. State St., Box 307, Trenton, NJ 08625, (609)
292-6260, **<njiway.net/state/darm/links/archives.html>**

NEW MEXICO ARCHIVES AND HISTORICAL SERVICES DIVISION
1205 Camino Carlos Rey, Santa Fe, NM 87507, (505) 476-7948,
<www.nmcpr.state.nm.us/archives/archives_hm.htm>

NEW YORK STATE ARCHIVES
Cultural Education Center, Albany, NY 12230,
(518) 474-8955, **<www.archives.nysed.gov>**

NORTH CAROLINA OFFICE OF ARCHIVES AND HISTORY
4610 Mail Service Center, Raleigh, NC 27699,
(919) 807-7280, **<www.history.ncdcr.gov>**

NORTH DAKOTA STATE ARCHIVES
612 E. Boulevard Ave., Bismarck, ND 58505,
(701) 328-2666, **<history.nd.gov/archives>**

OHIO
Ohio Historical Center, 1982 Velma Ave., Columbus, OH 43211,
(614) 297-2300, **<www.ohiohistory.org/resource/statearc>**

OKLAHOMA STATE ARCHIVES AND RECORDS MANAGEMENT
200 NE 18th St., Oklahoma City, OK 73105,
(405) 522-3579, **<www.odl.state.ok.us/oar>**

OREGON STATE ARCHIVES
800 Summer St. NE, Salem, OR 97310,
(503) 373-0701, **<arcweb.sos.state.or.us>**

PENNSYLVANIA
350 North St., Harrisburg, PA 17120,
(717) 783-3281, **<www.digitalarchives.state.pa.us>**

PUERTO RICO GENERAL ARCHIVE
(*ARCHIVO GENERAL DE PUERTO RICO*)
Instituto de Cultura, Box 9024184, San Juan, PR 00902,
(787) 725-1060, **<www.icp.gobierno.pr/agp>**

RHODE ISLAND STATE ARCHIVES
337 Westminster St., Providence, RI 02903,
(401) 222-2353, **<sos.ri.gov/archives>**

SOUTH CAROLINA DEPARTMENT OF ARCHIVES AND HISTORY
8301 Parklane Road, Columbia, SC 29223,
(803) 896-6100, **<scdah.sc.gov>**

SOUTH DAKOTA STATE ARCHIVES
900 Governors Drive, Pierre, SD 57501,
(605) 773-3804, **<history.sd.gov/archives>**

TENNESSEE STATE LIBRARY AND ARCHIVES
403 Seventh Ave. N, Nashville, TN 37243, (615) 741-2764,
<www.tennessee.gov/tsla>

TEXAS STATE LIBRARY AND ARCHIVES COMMISSION
Box 12927, Austin TX, 78711,
(512) 463-5455, **<www.tsl.state.tx.us>**

UTAH STATE ARCHIVES
300 South Rio Grande, Salt Lake City, UT 84101,
(801) 533-3535, **<www.archives.state.ut.us>**

VERMONT STATE ARCHIVES AND RECORDS ADMINISTRATION
1078 Route 2, Middlesex, Montpelier, VT 05633,
(802) 828-2308, **<vermont-archives.org>**

LIBRARY OF VIRGINIA
800 E. Broad St., Richmond, VA 23219,
(804) 692-3500, **<www.lva.virginia.gov>**

WASHINGTON, DC ARCHIVES
1300 Naylor Court, NW, Washington, DC 20001, (201)
671-1105, **<os.dc.gov/os/cwp/view,a,1207,q,585889.asp>**

WASHINGTON STATE ARCHIVES
Box 40238, Olympia WA 98504,
(360) 586-1492, **<www.sos.wa.gov/archives>**

WEST VIRGINIA STATE ARCHIVES
The Culture Center, 1900 Kanawha Blvd E.,
Charleston, WV 25305, (304) 558-0230,
<www.wvculture.org/history/wvsamenu.html>

WISCONSIN HISTORICAL SOCIETY
816 State St., Madison, WI 53706,
(608) 264-6460, **<www.wisconsinhistory.org>**

WYOMING STATE ARCHIVES
Barrett Building, 2301 Central Ave., Cheyenne, WY 82002,
(307) 777-7826, **<wyoarchives.state.wy.us>**

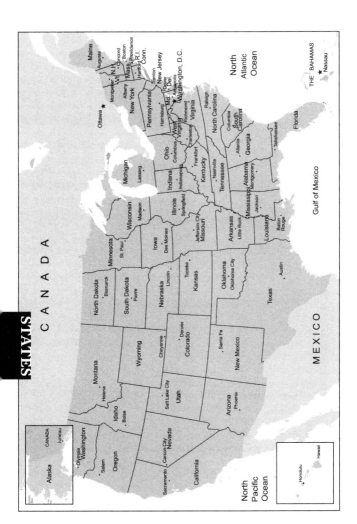

LIBRARIES & ARCHIVES

11 KEY GENEALOGY LIBRARIES AND ARCHIVES

ALLEN COUNTY PUBLIC LIBRARY
900 Library Plaza, Fort Wayne, IN 46802,
(260) 421-1200, **<www.acpl.lib.in.us>**

CLAYTON LIBRARY CENTER FOR GENEALOGICAL RESEARCH
5300 Caroline St., Houston, TX 77004,
(832) 393-2600, **<www.houstonlibrary.org/clayton>**

FAMILY HISTORY LIBRARY
35 N. West Temple St., Salt Lake City, UT 84150,
(866) 406-1830, **<www.familysearch.org>**;
find a local branch Family History Center near you at **<www.familysearch.org/eng/library/fhc/frameset_fhc.asp>**

DENVER PUBLIC LIBRARY
Western History and Genealogy, Central Library,
Level 5, 10 W. 14th Ave. Parkway, Denver, CO 80204,
(720) 865-1821, **<history.denverlibrary.org>**

LIBRARY OF CONGRESS
Thomas Jefferson Building, 101 Independence Ave. SE,
Washington, DC 20540, (202) 707-5000, **<loc.gov>**

MID-CONTINENT PUBLIC LIBRARY
MIDWEST GENEALOGY CENTER
3440 S. Lee's Summit Road, Independence, MO 64055,
(816) 252-7228, **<www.mcpl.lib.mo.us/genlh/mgc.htm>**

NATIONAL ARCHIVES AND RECORDS ADMINISTRATION
700 Pennsylvania Ave. NW, Washington, DC 20408,
(866) 272-6272, **<archives.gov>** (see regional locations on
the opposite page)

**NATIONAL SOCIETY DAUGHTERS OF
THE AMERICAN REVOLUTION LIBRARY**
1776 D St. NW, Washington, DC 20006,
(202) 628-1776, **<www.dar.org>**

**NEW ENGLAND HISTORIC GENEALOGICAL SOCIETY
RESEARCH LIBRARY**
99 Newbury St., Boston, MA 02116,
(888) 296-3447, **<www.newenglandancestors.org>**

THE NEW YORK PUBLIC LIBRARY
Irma and Paul Milstein Division of US History, Local History
and Genealogy, Room 121, 476 Fifth Ave., New York, NY
10018, (212) 930-0828, **<www.nypl.org>**

PUBLIC LIBRARY OF CINCINNATI AND HAMILTON COUNTY
800 Vine St., Cincinnati, OH 45202, (513) 369-6905,
<www.cincinnatilibrary.org>

NATIONAL ARCHIVES AND RECORDS ADMINISTRATION REGIONAL LOCATIONS

NARA REGIONAL ARCHIVES	STATES COVERED	PHYSICAL ADDRESS AND PHONE
CENTRAL PLAINS REGION (Kansas City) <archives.gov/central-plains>	Iowa, Kansas, Missouri, Nebraska; North Dakota and South Dakota before 1972	400 W. Pershing Road, Kansas City, MO 64108, (816) 268-8000
GREAT LAKES REGION (Chicago) <archives.gov/great-lakes>	Illinois, Indiana, Michigan, Minnesota, Ohio, Wisconsin	7358 S. Pulaski Road, Chicago, IL 60629, (773) 948-9001
MID-ATLANTIC REGION (Philadelphia) <archives.gov/midatlantic/public>	Delaware, Maryland, Pennsylvania, Virginia, West Virginia	900 Market St., Philadelphia, PA 19107, (215) 606-0100

NARA REGIONAL ARCHIVES	STATES COVERED	PHYSICAL ADDRESS AND PHONE
NORTHEAST REGION (New York) <archives.gov/northeast/nyc>	New York, New Jersey	201 Varick St., 12th Floor, New York, NY 10014, (866) 840-1752
NORTHEAST REGION (Pittsfield) <archives.gov/ northeast/pittsfield>	New England states	Silvio O. Conte National Records Center, 10 Conte Dr., Pittsfield, MA 01201, (413) 236-3600
NORTHEAST REGION (Boston) <archives.gov/ northeast/boston>	Connecticut, Maine, Massachusetts, New Hampshire, Rhode Island, Vermont	Frederick C. Murphy Federal Center, 380 Trapelo Road, Waltham, MA 02452, (781) 663-0130
PACIFIC ALASKA REGION (Anchorage) <archives.gov/ pacific-alaska/anchorage>	Alaska	654 W. Third Ave., Anchorage, AK 99501, (907) 261-7820,
PACIFIC ALASKA REGION (Seattle) <archives.gov/ pacific-alaska/seattle>	Idaho, Oregon, Washington	6125 Sand Point Way NE, Seattle, WA 98115, (206) 336-5115
PACIFIC REGION (Riverside, Calif.) <archives.gov/pacific/laguna>	Arizona, southern California, Nevada (Clark County only)	23123 Cajalco Road, Perris, CA 92570, (951) 956-2000
PACIFIC REGION (San Francisco) <archives.gov/ pacific/san-francisco>	Northern and central California, Hawaii, Nevada (except for Clark County)	1000 Commodore Dr., San Bruno, CA 94066, (650) 238-3501
ROCKY MOUNTAIN REGION (Denver) <archives.gov/ rocky-mountain>	Colorado, Montana, New Mexico, Utah, Wyoming; North Dakota and South Dakota after 1972	Denver Federal Center, Building 46 and 48, Denver, CO, 80225, (303) 407-5751
SOUTHEAST REGION (Atlanta) <archives.gov/southeast>	Alabama, Florida, Georgia, Kentucky, Mississippi, North Carolina, South Carolina, Tennessee	5780 Jonesboro Road, Morrow, GA 30260, (770) 968-2100
SOUTHWEST REGION (Fort Worth) <archives.gov/southwest>	Arkansas, Louisiana, Oklahoma, Texas	501 W. Felix St., Building 1, Fort Worth, TX 76115, (817) 831-5620

6 TIPS FOR REQUESTING
GENEALOGY RECORDS

1. Before you send a request, search the library's or archive's website to verify that it has the materials you need. If you can't find the information, e-mail or call the reference or genealogy desk and ask.

2. Look online for the library's instructions for requesting records. Follow them exactly, providing the information the library asks for about the ancestor who's the subject of the record, using the format specified (such as e-mail or a typed letter) and including any fees.

3. Double-check the name spellings and dates in your request to eliminate typos in names and dates (which can make the record impossible for a librarian to find). Include any nicknames or maiden names the ancestor may appear with.

4. Be realistic: Don't ask a librarian to search several years' worth of records, or to be able to hand you a completed pedigree chart. If the scope of your request goes beyond the time a librarian can devote to it, he or she may recommend you hire a private researcher.

5. If you don't receive a response within a couple of months, send a polite follow-up with a copy of your first request for reference.

6. As an alternative to requesting a record from a distant library, you may be able to borrow it through interlibrary loan on microfilm or in a book. Ask for assistance at your local library's reference or genealogy desk.

SEARCHING THE FHL CATALOG

The Family History Library (FHL) in Salt Lake City has 2.4 million rolls of microfilmed genealogy records and hundreds of thousands of microfiche, books, periodicals and electronic resources. The catalog has detailed descriptions of these materials. Print the description of the item you need and take it to a branch Family History Center to request a loan. You'll pay a small fee per microfilm roll or fiche, but printed books don't circulate. These search options will help you find what you need.

PLACE: Enter the name of a town, county (but don't include the word *county*), state or country for listings of books and microfilm for that location. Unlike most library catalogs, this one refers you to its standardized names: If you search on *Prussia*, you'll get a message "(See) Germany, *Preußen*." A search on *New Amsterdam* asks you to "(See) New York, New York (City)."

SURNAME: Enter a last name to find published and unpublished family histories.

KEYWORD: This search finds a word anywhere in the catalog listing. If you're searching on a common last name, add a place name or other keyword to narrow your search.

TITLE: Enter words from the title in any order (you needn't enter the entire title).

FILM/FICHE AND CALL NUMBER: Use these if you already have the film or book number.

AUTHOR: Look for records created by a person, government, business, church or society.

SUBJECT: This search uses Library of Congress subject headings.

SAMPLE RECORD REQUEST LETTER

Dear Sir or Madam:

I would like to order a copy of the marriage document for my grandparents, Michael John Mullinger and Jean Louise "Lou" Miller, who were married in Cincinnati, Hamilton County, Ohio, on Oct. 30, 1918. Michael was 23 at the time and Jean was 20.

Please also look under Mallinger, a common misspelling for Michael's surname.

As directed on your website, I have enclosed a check for the amount of $23.

Please mail the document to me at my mailing address, 123 Main St., Anywhere, USA, 12345. If you have any questions, you may contact me at (123) 456-7890 or via e-mail at **jrdoe@hotmail.com**.

Thank you very much for your assistance in this matter.

Sincerely,
John R. Mullinger

ONLINE DIGITIZED FAMILY HISTORIES

$ = subscription required to access most records

$ ANCESTRY.COM FAMILY AND LOCAL HISTORIES
<ancestry.com>

GOOGLE BOOKS
<books.google.com>

FAMILY HISTORY ARCHIVES
<www.lib.byu.edu/fhc/index.php>

HERITAGEQUEST ONLINE FAMILY AND LOCAL HISTORIES
<heritagequestonline.com> (available through
subscribing libraries)

MAKING OF AMERICA
<moa.cit.cornell.edu/moa> and **<moa.umdl.umich.edu>**

INTERNET ARCHIVE
<www.archive.org/details/texts>

$ WORLD VITAL RECORDS
<www.worldvitalrecords.com>

LIBRARIES

NAMES

TYPES OF SURNAMES

▷ **Patronymic**

The patronymic system bases a child's surname on the father's given name. This type of name is found throughout the world, but is especially common in Ireland, the Scottish highlands, Wales, Spain and Scandinavia. Various cultures have different prefixes and suffixes that may indicate a patronymic name. Those include:

ARMENIAN: -yan, -ian as in Hovnanian

DANISH: -sen as in Sorensen

DUTCH: -zoon, -sz, -dochter, -dr

ENGLISH: -son, Fitz-, -s as in Edwards; -ing as in Browning ("son of Brun")

GREEK: -opoulos as in Theodoropoulos ("son of Theodore")

HEBREW: ben as in Ben-Yehuda

IRISH: O' as in O'Hara ("grandson of Eaghra")

ITALIAN: De-, Di- as in DeCarlo

NORWEGIAN: -sen, -datter

PORTUGUESE: -az, -es as in Gomes ("son of Gomo")

ROMANIAN: -escu as in Tadescu

RUSSIAN: -ovna, -ovich as in Pavlovich

POLISH: -wicz as in Danielewicz

SCOTTISH: -son, Fitz-, Mac, Mc as in McCall ("son of Cachal")

SPANISH: -es, -ez as in Alvarez ("son of Alva")

SWEDISH: -dotter; -son as in Olafson ("son of Olaf")

TURKISH: -oglu as in Turnacioglu

UKRAINIAN: -ovich, -ovna, -enko as in Kovalenko

WELSH: -ap, -ab, p- as in Upjohn ("son of John"), b- as in Bowen ("son of Owen")

▷ Place-Based

This type of name is derived from a nearby geographical or natural feature such as a hill, brook, valley, bridge; a place of origin; or ownership of a manor or village. Place-based names are common in England, Germany and France. Examples include:

CHINESE: Li ("plum tree"), Wong ("field," "wide sea" or "ocean")

DUTCH: Roosevelt ("rose field"), Van Pelt ("from Pelt")

ENGLISH: names with suffixes -ton, -wick, ley, -thorpe, -ham, -land and -ford

FRENCH: Cassell ("chateau" or "castle"), De Long ("from the large place")

GERMAN: Steinbach ("stony brook"); names with -er added to a locality, as in Berliner ("from Berlin")

ITALIAN: Lombard, Lombardi, Lombardo ("from Lombardy"), Napoli ("from Naples")

POLISH: Bielski ("from Bielsk"), Wisniewski ("from Wiznia")

PORTUGUESE: Ferreira ("from Ferreira," meaning "iron mine" or "workshop"), Teixeira ("place of yew trees")

SPANISH: Cortez ("court" or "town"), Morales ("mulberry tree"), Navarro ("the plain among hills")

FROM FLANDERS: Flanders, Fleming

FROM ENGLAND: England, Englander, Engel or Engelman (in German), Inglis (in Scotland)

FROM GERMANY: Allemand (in France)

▷ Occupational
This type of name is derived from an occupation, such as Smith, Miller, Taylor and Clark. Occupational surnames are among the most common surnames in the United States.

▷ Nickname-Based
These names describe personal appearance (stature, hair, eyes, complexion), characteristics (strong, bold, brave), financial status, habits or skills. They may be combined with patronymics; for example, the Italian D'Onofrio ("son of a giant"). Nickname-based names are common in Italy and Portugal. For example, names that mean "poor" are Powers or Poor (English), Scholl (German) or Chudak (Czech or Slovak).

---

16 MOST COMMON US SURNAMES IN 2000

1. Smith	**5.** Jones	**9.** Rodríguez	**13.** Taylor
2. Johnson	**6.** Miller	**10.** Wilson	**14.** Thomas
3. Williams	**7.** Davis	**11.** Martinez	**15.** Hernández
4. Brown	**8.** García	**12.** Anderson	**16.** Moore

TIPS FOR RESEARCHING
COMMON SURNAMES

1. Learn as much identifying information about the ancestor as possible, such as where he lived and his birth year and place, to rule out others with the same name.

2. Anchor the person with a spouse, child or other person who has an uncommon name.

3. Make a chronology of the person's life events to compare with records of same-named individuals.

CULTURAL NAMING TRADITIONS

FRENCH: Multiple Christian names; nicknames may be used instead of given names.

DUTCH: Many surnames or middle names were patronymic until 1811, when permanent surnames were required.

GERMAN: First name may be a "prefix name" given at baptism; the middle name was the *Rufnahmen* ("call name") the individual used. For example, Johann Christian Miller may have been known as Christian Miller.

GREEK: First son named after paternal grandfather, first daughter named after paternal grandmother, second son named after maternal grandfather and so on. For middle initials, children took the first letter of the father's given name. Married women changed the middle initial to the first letter of the husband's name.

HUNGARIAN: Family name commonly goes before the given name. Women often add the suffix -né to the husband's name;

for example, Great-grandma Erzébet might be in records as Kovács Mátyásné (Mrs. Mátyás Kovács, or Matthew's wife).

IRISH: Given names tend to repeat over generations.

ITALIAN: First son named after paternal grandfather; first daughter, after paternal grandmother; second son, after maternal grandfather; second daughter, after maternal grandmother. Third son and daughter named after the parents. Children may be named after deceased siblings (necronymics).

JEWISH: Ashkenazi generally name children after deceased relatives; Sephardim often name children after living grandparents, with first son after the paternal grandfather, first daughter after maternal grandmother, and so on.

POLISH: Catholics often named a child after a saint whose feast day was on or near the birth or baptism.

PORTUGUESE, SPANISH: Prefixes such as *de la* were often added to surnames. Married women typically kept their maiden names. Children took both the father's and mother's last names, using the father's surname as the family name. For example, when Julia Jimenez Montero marries Alejandro Ignacio Perez, she remains Julia Jimenez Montero, possibly adding her husband's family name to become Julia Jimenez Montero de Perez. In Spain, their daughter, Marta, would become Marta Perez Jimenez. In Portugal, where the second surname is the man's family name, she would be Marta Jimenez Perez.

SCANDINAVIAN: Patronymic surnames are common; permanent surnames became official 1901 in Sweden and 1923 in Norway. Norwegians also often used a second last name based on their farm: Olav Petersen Dal became Olav Petersen Li after moving to the Li farm. Men may have taken different surnames while in the military, and may have changed them back later.

SCOTTISH: The first son was named after the paternal grandfather; second son, after the maternal grandfather; third son, after the father; fourth son, after the father's brother; first daughter, after the paternal grandmother; second daughter, after the maternal grandmother; third daughter, after the mother; fourth daughter, after the mother's sister.

NICKNAMES AND VARIATIONS FOR POPULAR FEMALE NAMES

ABIGAIL: Abby, Gail, Nabby

BARBARA: Babs, Barb, Barbie, Bobbie, Bonnie

CAROLYN/CAROLINE: Caddie, Callie, Carol, Carrie, Lena, Lynn

CATHERINE: Cathryn, Cathy, Katharine, Kathleen, Karen, Katie, Kay, Kit, Kittie, Rhynie, Rina, Trina

CHRISTINE/CHRISTINA: Chris, Christiana, Crissy, Christy, Ina, Kissy, Kit, Kris, Krissy, Kristina, Kristine, Tina, Xina

ELAINE/ELEANOR: Elena, Ella, Ellen, Ellie, Elsie, Helen, Lana, Lainie, Lena, Leonora, Nell, Nellie, Nora

ELIZABETH: Bess, Bessie, Bet, Beth, Betsy, Betty, Bitsy, Eli, Eliza, Elsie, Ibby, Libby, Lisa, Lish, Liz, Liza, Lizbet, Lizzie, Tess

JOANNA/JOHANNAH: Hannah, Jo, Joan, Joanie, Jody, Josie

MARGARET: Margareta, Magdelene, Daisy, Greta, Madge, Maggie, Marge, Margie, Margo, Meg, Midge, Peg, Peggy

MARY/MARIA: Mae, Mamie, May, Mattie, Mimi, Molly, Polly

MELISSA: Lisa, Lissa, Mel, Missy

SARAH: Sally

SUSAN/SUSANNA: Anna, Hannah, Nan, Nanny, Sue, Sukey, Susie, Suzanne, Suze

THERESA: Terrie, Tess, Tessie, Tessa, Thursa, Tracy

VERONICA: Franky, Frony, Ron, Ronnie, Ronna, Vonnie

VIRGINIA: Ginger, Ginny, Jane, Jennie, Virgy

NICKNAMES AND VARIATIONS FOR POPULAR MALE NAMES

ALEXANDER: Al, Alastair, Alex, Alisdair, Alistair, Eleck, Sandy, Zan

ANDREW: Andy, Drew

BENJAMIN: Ben, Bennie, Benjy, Jamie

CHARLES: Carl, Charlie, Charley, Chick, Chuck

EDWARD/EDMUND: Ed, Eddie, Eddy, Ned, Ted, Teddy

FREDERICK/ALFRED: Al, Fred, Freddie, Freddy, Fritz, Rick

JAMES/JAMESON: Jamie, Jem, Jim, Jimi, Jimmy, Mamey

JONATHAN: Eon, Ian, Jack, Jock, John, Johannes, Johnny, Jon, Nathan

LAWRENCE/LAURENCE: Larry, Lon, Lonny, Lorne, Lorry

MATTHEW/MATTHIAS: Matt, Matty, Thias, Thys

MICHAEL: Micah, Mick, Mickey, Mickie, Micky, Mike

PATRICK: Paddy, Pat, Pate

RICHARD: Dick, Dickie, Dickson, Rich, Rick, Ricky

ROBERT: Bob, Bobby, Dob, Dobbin, Rob, Robbie, Robin, Robby, Rupert

THOMAS: Tam, Tom, Thom, Tomi, Tommie, Tommy

WILLIAM: Bill, Billy, Will, Willy

ZACHARIAH/ZACHARY: Zach, Zachy, Zack, Zak, Zeke

NAMES

ONLINE GENEALOGY

MAJOR GENEALOGY RESOURCE SITES

$ = subscription required to access most records

ACCESSGENEALOGY <www.accessgenealogy.com>: millions of records from most US states

AFRIGENEAS <www.afrigeneas.com>: free slave records, a surnames database, death and marriage databases and census schedules

ONLINE GENEALOGY

$ ANCESTRY.COM <ancestry.com>: US census records; many Canadian, England and Wales censuses; US passenger arrivals; military records; vital-records indexes from various US states, Canada and the United Kingdom; family and local history books; city directories; yearbooks; newspapers; user-contributed family trees (note that most Ancestry.com content is available free at libraries that subscribe to Ancestry Library Edition)

$ ARCHIVES.COM <archives.com>: US census indexes; US and Canadian vital records indexes, passenger indexes, military records indexes, living person search, family tree builder

BUREAU OF LAND MANAGEMENT GENERAL LAND OFFICE RECORDS <www.glorecords.blm.gov>: more than 3 million federal land title records spanning 1820 to 1908, plus Colorado, Idaho, Montana, South Dakota and North Dakota Master Title Plats, surveyors' field notes, bounty land warrants issued and more

CANADIAN GENEALOGY CENTRE <www.collectionscanada. gc.ca/genealogy/index-e.html>: research guides to Canadian records, census records, passenger records and indexes, immigration indexes, military indexes, land records indexes, photos and more

CASTLE GARDEN <castlegarden.org>: names and basic details for 11 million New York immigrants arriving between 1820 and 1892, as well as some later passengers

CIVIL WAR SOLDIERS & SAILORS SYSTEM <www.itd.nps.gov/cwss>: 6.3 million names of Union and Confederate soldiers from 44 states and territories, regimental histories and battle histories

CYNDI'S LIST <cyndislist.com>: links to more than 275,000 genealogy websites in 180-plus categories

DAUGHTERS OF THE AMERICAN REVOLUTION <www.dar.org>: searchable databases including the DAR Genealogical Research System, which contains information on ancestors submitted in member applications

DISTANTCOUSIN.COM <www.distantcousin.com>: more than 6 million records from city directories, school alumni lists, vital records, military records and obituaries

ELLIS ISLAND <ellisisland.org>: 22 million records of passenger arrivals through the port of New York from 1892 to 1924

FAMILYSEARCH <www.familysearch.org>: 1880 US census index, 1881 Canadian and British Isles census indexes, the Social Security Death Index, pedigree databases, vital records index, and 25,000-plus digitized publications

FAMILYSEARCH RECORD SEARCH PILOT <pilot.familysearch.org> and FAMILYSEARCH BETA <fsbeta.familysearch.org>: 1850 through 1880, 1900 and 1920 US census records or indexes; US vital records indexes; 1851, 1871, 1891 Canadian census indexes; Mexico 1930 census; Mexican marriages and church records; civil registrations and church records from around the world and more

FIND A GRAVE <www.findagrave.com>: more than 44 million grave records, many accompanied by photos

$ FINDMYPAST.CO.UK <findmypast.co.uk>: British birth, marriage and death records; 1841 to 1911 English and Welsh censuses; military records; outbound passenger lists, living person search, family tree building

$ FOOTNOTE <footnote.com>: military records; newspapers; city directories; Southern Claims Commission files; naturalizations; passport applications; 1860 and 1930 US censuses (other censuses are being added); Indian reservation censuses; member pages about individuals and events and more (ask your library if it subscribes to the institutional version of Footnote)

$ GENEALOGYBANK <www.genealogybank.com>: historical newspapers and books; 130 million obituaries back to 1977; the Social Security Death Index; and historical documents including military casualty lists, the US Congressional Serial Set and American State Papers

HERITAGEQUESTONLINE <www.heritagequestonline.com> (available through subscribing libraries): US censuses from 1790 to 1930 (some lack indexes); the Periodical Source Index; Revolutionary War pension and bounty land warrant applications; Freedman's Bank records; and the US Serial Set

IMMIGRANT SHIPS TRANSCRIBERS GUILD <www.immigrant ships.net>: volunteer-submitted transcriptions of more than 11,000 passenger records

JEWISHGEN <www.jewishgen.org>: Family Finder surname database, ShtetlSeeker, Holocaust Database, Worldwide Burial Registry, Yizkor Book Project Database, country-specific databases and more

LIBRARY OF CONGRESS <loc.gov>: the American Memory collection, digitized records and images, American Slave Narratives, National Union Catalog of Manuscript Collections, and Chronicling America newspaper collection (also at **<chroniclingamerica.loc.gov>**)

MYHERITAGE <myheritage.com>: millions of family websites (there's a fee for premium hosting services), genealogy metasearch, free downloadable family tree-building software

NATIONAL ARCHIVES AND RECORDS ADMINISTRATION <archives.gov>: research guides; Access to Archival Databases collection with more than 85 million listings in indexes to military, passenger and other records; and the Archival Research Catalog with indexes to 6.3 million records (includes 153,000 digitized documents or photos)

NATIONWIDE GRAVESITE LOCATOR <gravelocator.cem. va.gov>: US burials of veterans and their families in VA National Cemeteries, state veterans cemeteries, various other military and Department of Interior cemeteries, as well as some private cemeteries

$ NEWENGLANDANCESTORS <www.newenglandancestors. org>: more than 2,400 databases encompassing 110 million names, including vital records, early American newspapers, court records, military records, Sanborn fire-insurance maps, research journal indexes and more

NEWSPAPER ABSTRACTS <www.newspaperabstracts.com>: 69,000-plus pages of abstracts and extracts from historical newspapers, focusing on obituaries, births, marriages, deaths, court notices, land sales and tax notices

OLIVETREEGENEALOGY: 1,500 free ship-list transcriptions, plus links to off-site passenger lists

ONE-STEP WEB PAGES <stevemorse.org>: enhanced searching of databases at Ellis Island, Castle Garden, Ancestry.com and more; enumeration district finders and other tools

$ ONEGREATFAMILY <www.onegreatfamily.com>: more than 190 million searchable names in members' family trees

ROOTSWEB <rootsweb.ancestry.com>: records transcriptions, the WorldConnect pedigree file, a surname database, 161,000 message boards and nearly 30,000 mailing lists

THESHIPSLIST <www.theshipslist.com>: passenger lists, immigration reports, newspaper records, shipwreck information, ship pictures and descriptions, and more

USGENWEB <usgenweb.org>: umbrella site for volunteer-run state and county pages, as well as several special projects; records include transcriptions of censuses, tombstone inscriptions, church records and more

WESTERN STATES HISTORICAL MARRIAGE RECORDS INDEX <abish.byui.edu/specialcollections/westernstates/search.cfm>: index of nearly 700,000 nuptials from Arizona, Idaho, Nevada, California, western Colorado, Montana, Oregon, Utah, eastern Washington and Wyoming

$ WORLD VITAL RECORDS <www.worldvitalrecords.com>: more than 1.2 billion genealogy records, including digitized books; abstracts and transcriptions from books; digitized newspapers; pedigree charts and family group sheets; censuses of England and Wales and more

GENEALOGY SOCIAL NETWORKING SITES

FAMILYLINK <www.familylink.com>: From the company behind GenealogyWise, this app can work with Facebook or independently. Create a profile and find relatives already on the network, or invite your e-mail contacts and Facebook friends.

FAMIVA <www.famiva.com>: Build family trees, share photos and collaborate.

GENEALOGYWISE <www.genealogywise.com>: Like a genealogy-only Facebook, with member profiles, groups based on research interests or surnames, photo albums, blogs and chats.

GENETREE <www.genetree.com>: A social networking site where you can build a family tree with DNA test results.

GENI <geni.com>: Network with family, build a family tree, invite relatives to collaborate and merge your research with theirs (basic accounts are free).

KINCAFE <kincafe.com>: A free site that lets you collaborate on building family trees, sharing photos and keeping a family calendar.

MYFAMILY.COM <myfamily.com>: An Ancestry.com site where you create a family home page with pictures, events and ancestral information (basic sites are free; paid plans offer more storage).

MYHERITAGE.COM <myheritage.com>: Lets you create a free family website in a range of languages (you'll pay a fee for enhanced sites).

WERELATE <www.werelate.org>: A wiki for genealogy, with pages on more than 2 million people and families.

BOOLEAN SEARCH TERMS

Use these key Boolean "operators" to narrow your online search engine results and eliminate unwanted matches. Remember that capitalization doesn't matter in almost all online searches.

AND: Specifies that the term following it must appear in each search result: a search on *Selby and Massachusetts* returns only pages with the words *Selby* and *Massachusetts.*

OR: Searches for either of two terms, as in *Dupree OR Dupray OR Dupre OR Dupreen genealogy* (the OR operator must be capitalized in Google searches). The pipe symbol does the same thing: *Dupree | Dupray | Dupre | Dupreen genealogy.*

NEAR: Finds web pages in which two words appear near each other: *"john henry" near "Connecticut."* Neither Google nor Yahoo! recognizes this operator, but you can fake it with Google by using the GAPS tool (short for Google API Proximity Search) available at **<www.staggernation.com/cgi-bin/gaps.cgi>**.

QUOTATION MARKS (""): Use to specify that the search term must appear as an exact phrase in every search result. For example, a search on *"Robert Selby"* returns pages with the words *Robert* and *Selby* side by side in that order.

PLUS SIGN (+): Acts like the operator *and*; for example, a search on *Selby + Massachusetts* returns pages with the words *Selby* and *Massachusetts.*

MINUS SIGN (-): Specifies that the term following it must not appear in search results. For example, search on *Reese -peanut* to find pages with the word *Reese* but not *peanut* (useful for eliminating candy results from your Reese surname search).

GOOGLE SEARCH HACKS

▷ **Search Syntaxes**

SITE: To search for content on a specific website, just include *site:plus* the domain name, as in *harriet railey site:rootsweb. ancestry.com*. Use this to focus on particular types of sites, as in *site:.gov* or *site:.org*.

URL: Don't know the exact domain of the site you want to search? Try *inurl:* to find pages on sites with the word genealogy in their Web address: *railey inurl:genealogy*.

TITLE: Sites usually put their names in the title bar that appears at the top of your browser, so use Google's *intitle:* syntax to find "Smithers Family Genealogy" or "Barb's Smithers Home Page." Just type *intitle:smithers genealogy*.

▷ **Search Tools**

DICTIONARY: Wondering what it means if your ancestor died intestate? Type *define:intestate* to learn he didn't leave a will.

CALCULATOR: Simply enter an equation into the search box, using * to multiply and / to divide. If your great-grandfather's property was 450x160 feet, input *450*160=* to get the square footage of 72,000.

UNIT CONVERSION: This works for various height, weight and mass measurements. Enter *72000 sq ft in acres* to learn Great-grandpa owned 1.6 acres of land.

CURRENCY CONVERSION: How much will that record request from the British national archives end up costing you? Just model your search query after the following (substituting the appropriate fee amount in pounds): *10 british pounds in us dollars*. You can even abbreviate this as *10 gpb in usd*. You'll find out the fee's equivalent in dollars.

AREA CODES: You've located a phone number for someone who may be your distant cousin, but you aren't sure where she lives. Enter the area code *240* to discover she resides in western Maryland.

GOOGLE QUICK LINKS

ALERTS
<google.com/alerts>

BOOK SEARCH
<books.google.com>

CALENDAR
<google.com/calendar>

DESKTOP
<desktop.google.com>

DOCS
<google.com/docs>

EARTH
<earth.google.com>

GMAIL
<mail.google.com>

IGOOGLE
<google.com/ig>

IMAGE SEARCH
<images.google.com>

LANGUAGE TOOLS
<google.com/language_tools>

MAPS
<maps.google.com>

NOTEBOOK
<google.com/notebook>

PATENT SEARCH
<google.com/patents>

PICASA
<picasa.google.com>

READER
<google.com/reader>

TOOLBAR

FAMILYSEARCH DATABASE TRICKS

Access the following databases from **<www.familysearch. org/eng/search/frameset_search.asp>**.

ANCESTRAL FILE: You can search this database for relatives who aren't in your direct line. From the Ancestral File search form, type in the father's full name and at least the mother's first name. The search will return a list of their children, each linked to the child's individual record page.

INTERNATIONAL GENEALOGICAL INDEX (IGI): Batch numbers can help you jump from one ancestor's record to other people who were entered into the database at the same time from the same place—these may be relatives or family friends of your ancestors.

Once you've done a successful IGI search, click the batch number in the lower left corner of the screen. That brings up a new IGI search on the batch number. Click Search to see all individuals entered into the IGI in the same batch.

PEDIGREE RESOURCE FILE: Look near the bottom of an ancestor's individual record page for the Submission Search number. Click on the number to return to the search form with the number automatically entered in the Submission Number field. Type your ancestor's surname in the surname field and click Search for a list of people with the surname whose records were submitted by the same individual.

ANCESTRY.COM HOT KEYS

Using these keyboard shortcuts to save time when searching on Ancestry.com and browsing your search results.

N See a new search form pop up in browser.

R See a search form pre-populated with data you just searched on.

P> Move down the list of search results (hold down both keys at the same time).

P< Move up the list of search results (hold down both keys at the same time).

J Move down the list of search results.

K Move up the list of research results.

COMPUTING

COMPUTER KEYBOARD SHORTCUTS

What's the fastest and easiest route to quicker comput-
ing? Mastering keyboard shortcuts for common commands.
Shortcuts for PCs and Macs are listed in the table below (the
Mac's Command key is the one with the apple icon).

FUNCTION	PC	MAC
Open a file	Control-O	Command-O
Close a file	Control-W	Command-W
Quit a program	Control-Q	Command-Q
Create a **new file** or folder	Control-N	Command-N
Save	Control-S	Command-S
Print	Control-P	Command-P
Find	Control-F	Command-F
Select all the data in a document	Control-A	Command-A
Copy selected text	Control-C	Command-C
Cut selected text	Control-X	Command-X
Paste copied or cut text	Control-V	Command-V
Boldface selected text	Control-B	Command-B
Italicize selected text	Control-I	Command-I
Change selected text to **upper-or lowercase**	Shift-F3	Shift-F3
Increase size of selected text	Control-Shift->	Command-Shift->
Decrease size of selected text	Control-Shift-<	Command-Shift-<
Undo	Control-Z	Command-Z

COMPUTER FILE FORMAT GUIDE

We've all received a computer file we didn't know how to open. The secret to identifying a compatible software program lies in the three- or four-letter extension at the end of the file name. This glossary will help you unscramble those mystery letters and identify the format for the file you've received.

AVI: Audio Video Interleave. Most often played on Apple QuickTime or Windows Media Player, this format for sound and video clips is becoming obsolete.

BMP: Windows bitmap. These image files tend to be large because they are uncompressed; they have wide acceptance in all Windows systems.

DOC: If you use Microsoft Word to type genealogy notes or correspondence, the resulting files are DOCs.

DOCX: The Microsoft Word file extension if you have the latest version for the PC or Mac. Someone with an older version will need to download a file converter or use an online utility to read a DOCX file.

FDB: The native file format for Legacy Family Tree genealogy software.

FTW: The native file format for Family Tree Maker genealogy software.

GED: GEDCOM (short for Genealogical Data Communications). When genealogists who use different family tree programs want to share their family files, they can convert their data to this standard file format that any genealogy software can open.

GIF: Graphics Interchange Format. Most image-editing software, such as Adobe Photoshop Elements or Jasc Paint Shop Pro, can open this graphics format for still and animated images. Excellent for simple images that contain text, it's most often used for web graphics with a small number of colors (not photos).

HTML: Hypertext Markup Language. This is the predominant programming language for web pages. Open an HTML file in Internet Explorer or another web browser to view the "finished" page; use an HTML or plain-text editor such as Notepad to see or change the coding.

JPG: Also JPEG, it's short for Joint Photographic Experts Group. JPG has become the most widely used format for static photographic images because it can display millions of colors. Any image-editing software can read a JPG.

MOV: Apple Quicktime Movie. MOV is probably the most common multimedia format for saving video or movie files. It's compatible with both Macintosh and Windows platforms.

MP3: One of the most popular audio formats, MP3 compresses sound clips into small files without losing quality. You can play MP3s on a portable device such as an iPod, or software such as iTunes and Real Player.

MPEG: Moving Picture Experts Group. Any Mac or Windows video player can read this video format, popular for creating movies that get distributed over the Internet. The related MPEG-4 format uses separate compression for audio and video tracks.

PAF: Data files created by Personal Ancestral File software. Several other genealogy programs, including Family Tree Maker, Legacy and RootsMagic, can import PAF files directly.

PDF: Portable Document Format. Created to ease document exchanges, PDF lets you use the free Adobe Reader to view a file exactly as it was designed, even without the program that created it.

PJC: The extension for files created by The Master Genealogist software, which can directly import the native file formats of most popular genealogy programs.

PNG: Portable Network Graphics. Developed as a replacement for the GIF format—and used for the same types of files—PNG does a better job of compressing files, resulting in a smaller-size files of equal quality. Most image-editing software can open PNG files.

PSD: Photoshop Document. Adobe Photoshop's native format allows for preservation of layers, masks and profiles used in image editing.

RAW: Certain digital cameras support this "raw" image format, which uses nearly lossless compression while still being smaller than TIFF format photos. It is sometimes called DNG (Adobe's Digital Negative format).

RMG: RootsMagic genealogy software's native file format.

SIT: A file compressed by StuffIt software. SIT files were originally usable only by Macs, but now Windows can create and open these files, too. Note that both SIT and ZIP (see the next page) shrink the size of other file formats for easier exchanging or archiving. You can click the SIT file icon to "unstuff" the files, but you'll still need the applicable software to view the original files.

TGA: Truevision Advanced Raster Graphics Adapter; used for raster images, such as in video games.

TIFF: Tagged Image File Format. Good for bitmap (pixel-based) images, such as photographs. Since TIFF produces large files, it's excellent if the end use is print (not web) or archival.

TXT: Refers to plain-text files with little formatting; for example, no bold or italics. This format is most commonly used in simple text editors such as Windows Notepad and Mac TextEdit, but you can open them in almost any program that that can read a plain-text file (including word processors), making them good for file sharing.

WAV: Short for waveform, WAV is the standard format for storing audio on a PC. You can play WAV files on Windows or Mac in a program such as Windows Media Player or iTunes.

WMA: Windows Media Audio. WMA produces smaller files than WAV, but you can listen to them on similar software, including Windows Media Player and RealPlayer.

WMV: Windows Media Video. Used for internet video, this file format must be read with Windows Media Player or an application such as RealPlayer. Flip4Mac offers conversion for Mac users.

ZIP: Similar to SIT, ZIP format uses Zip compression to compress a document or documents into one smaller file for sharing or archiving. Windows users can create ZIP files using a program such as WINZIP, while Mac OSX users can simply Control-click a file and select Create Archive of [file name].

GENEALOGY DESKTOP SOFTWARE GUIDE

SOFTWARE	PC/MAC	FREE TRIAL/ DEMO	WEBSITE
Ancestral Quest	PC	Yes	\<www.ancquest.com\>
Brother's Keeper	PC	Yes	\<www.bkwin.com\>
Family Historian	PC	Yes	\<www.family-historian.co.uk\>
Family Tree Heritage	PC	No	\<www.individualsoftware.com/software/genealogy_family_trees/family_tree_heritage\>
Family Tree Legends	PC	Yes	\<www.familytreelegends.com\>
Family Tree Maker	PC (a Mac version is in production)	No	\<www.familytreemaker.com\>
Family Trees Quick & Easy	PC	No	\<www.individualsoftware.com/software/genealogy_family_trees/family_trees_quick_easy\>
GEDitCOM	Mac	Yes	\<www.geditcom.com\>
Genbox Family History	PC	Yes	\<www.genbox.com\>
Heredis Mac X	Mac	Yes	\<www.myheredis.com\>
Heritage Family Tree Deluxe	PC	No	\<www.individualsoftware.com/software/genealogy_family_trees/heritage_family_tree\>
iFamily for Leopard	Mac	Yes	\<www.ifamilyforleopard.com\>
Legacy Family Tree Deluxe	PC	Yes	\<www.legacyfamilytree.com\>
MacFamilyTree	Mac	Yes	\<www.synium.de/products/macfamilytree\>
The Master Genealogist	PC	Yes	\<www.whollygenes.com/tmg.htm\>
Personal Ancestral File	PC	Yes	\<www.familysearch.org/eng/paf\>
Reunion	Mac	Yes	\<www.leisterpro.com\>
RootsMagic	PC	Yes	\<www.rootsmagic.com\>

GENEALOGY COMPUTING RESOURCES

CYNDI'S LIST: GEDCOM
<www.cyndislist.com/gedcom.htm>
Links to resources for creating and using GEDCOM files.

CYNDI'S LIST: SOFTWARE AND COMPUTERS
<www.cyndislist.com/software.htm>
Links to genealogy software-related websites.

FAMILYTREEMAGAZINE.COM SOFTWARE GUIDE
<familytreemagazine.com/
ResearchToolkit/SoftwareGuide>
List of genealogy programs and basic facts about each.

GENFORUM.COM: GENEALOGY SOFTWARE
AND THE INTERNET
<genforum.com/general/#computers>
Message boards for getting help with software questions.

GENSOFTREVIEWS
<www.gensoftreviews.com>
User reviews of genealogy software, utilities and tools.

MACGENEALOGY.ORG
<www.macgenealogy.org>
Mac genealogy software news and information.

MOBILEGENEALOGY.COM
<www.mobilegenealogy.com>
News and reviews on software for mobile devices.

ROOTSWEB GENEALOGY MAILING LISTS: SOFTWARE
<lists.rootsweb.ancestry.com/index/other/Software>
Subscribe to the list for your genealogy software
program for help and tips from other users.

GENEALOGY SMART PHONE APPS

▷ **Pedigree Viewers**

FAMVIEWER

Aster Software

<www.apple.com/ca/iphone/apps-for-iphone>

Supports multiple GEDCOM files and large databases. Works with iPhone and iPod Touch.

SHRUBS

Benoît Bousquet

<software.benoitbousquet.com/view.php?app=shrubs>

Works with GEDCOM files and has a text display. You can take notes in person view. Works with iPhone and iPod Touch.

▷ **Tree-Editors**

ANCESTRY.COM TREE TO GO

Ancestry.com **<landing.ancestry.com/iphone>**

Edit and upload photos to an Ancestry.com family tree. Works with iPhone and iPod touch. Best for trees with fewer than 2,000 people.

GEDVIEW

David A. Knight

<www.ritter.demon.co.uk/Projects/gedview.html>

Offers individual and family views. Works with GEDCOM files and supports multiple databases. Compatible with iPhone and iPod devices.

MOBILEFAMILYTREE

Synium Software GmbH

<www.synium.de/products/mobilefamilytree>

Requires MacFamilyTree software, from the same company. Compatible with iPhone and iPod Touch.

MOBILETREE
\<mobiletree.me\>
Search, view and edit files on a FamilySearch Family Tree from an iPhone or an iPod Touch.

POCKET GENEALOGIST
Northern Hills Software
\<www.pocketgenealogist.com\>
For phones that run the Windows Mobile operating system.

REUNION FOR IPHONE AND IPOD
Leister Productions
\<www.apple.com/ca/iphone/apps-for-iphone\>
Requires Reunion for Macintosh version 9.09 or higher.

▷ **Other**
FAMCAM
FamilyLink
\<www.apple.com/ca/iphone/apps-for-iphone\>
Share photos with family from your iPhone or iPod Touch.

GENEALOGY GEMS
\<www.apple.com/ca/iphone/apps-for-iphone\>
Access recordings of the free Genealogy Gems podcast. Works with iPhone and iPod Touch.

TRACES OF THE PAST
Truscape Solutions
\<www.apple.com/ca/iphone/apps-for-iphone\>
Searches sites including FamilySearch, Footnote, Ellis Island and more (some require subscriptions and/or registration). Works with iPhone and iPod Touch.

CENSUS

MOST COMMON ANCESTRIES IN THE 2000 US CENSUS

ANCESTRY	NUMBER OF PEOPLE	PERCENTAGE OF POPULATION
German	42.8 million	15.2
Irish	30.5 million	10.8
African-American	24.9 million	8.8
English	24.5 million	8.7
American	20.2 million	7.2
Mexican	18.4 million	6.5
Italian	15.6 million	5.6
Polish	9.0 million	3.2
French	8.3 million	3
American Indian	7.9 million	2.8
Scottish	4.9 million	1.7
Dutch	4.5 million	1.6
Norwegian	4.5 million	1.6
Scots-Irish	4.3 million	1.5
Swedish	4.0 million	1.4
White	3.8 million	1.4
Puerto Rico	2.7 million	.9
Russian	2.7 million	.9
Hispanic	2.5 million	.9
French Canadian	2.3 million	.8
Chinese	2.3 million	.8
Spanish	2.2 million	.8

Table reflects respondents' self-identified ancestry groups. About 500 ancestries were reported.

HISTORICAL US POPULATION IN MILLIONS

1790 3.9	**1870** 38.6	**1940** 132.2
1800 5.2	**1880** 50.2	**1950** 151.3
1810 7	**1890** 63	**1960** 179.3
1820 10	**1900** 76.2	**1970** 203.2
1830 12.8	**1910** 92.2	**1980** 226.5
1840 17	**1920** 106	**1990** 248.7
1850 23	**1930** 123.2	**2000** 281.4
1860 31.4		

US CENSUS RECORD WEBSITES

$ = subscription required to access most records

$ ANCESTRY.COM <ancestry.com>: all extant population census records and every-name indexes

ANCESTRY LIBRARY EDITION: all extant population census records and every-name indexes (available at subscribing libraries)

$ ARCHIVES.COM <archives.com>: partial index and records for 1870, 1880, 1900 and 1910 censuses; index for 1860 and 1930 censuses (additional indexes are being added)

FAMILYSEARCH <www.familysearch.org>: 1880 every-name index and transcription

FAMILYSEARCH RECORD SEARCH PILOT <pilot.familysearch.org> and **FAMILYSEARCH BETA <fsbeta.familysearch.org>:** records and every-name indexes for 1850 to 1880 and 1900; index only for 1920

$ FOOTNOTE <footnote.com>: records and every-name indexes for 1860, 1930, and portions of 1900 to 1920 (this site is adding all US census records)

HERITAGEQUEST ONLINE <www.heritagequestonline.com>: record images for all US censuses; head-of-household indexes for 1790 to 1820, 1860 to 1920, and part of 1930 (available through subscribing libraries)

USGENWEB ARCHIVES CENSUS PROJECT <usgwarchives.net/ census>: volunteer-submitted indexes and some images of census records from various places and years

ONLINE CENSUS SEARCH TIPS

READ THE SITE'S SEARCH TIPS AND INSTRUCTIONS. They'll reveal tricks such as using wildcard symbols to find alternate spellings of your ancestors' names.

SEARCH A SITE'S INDIVIDUAL CENSUS DATABASES ONE AT A TIME. Those customized search forms often let you include terms not allowed in a site's global search, letting you better target your search.

MAKE SURE THE COLLECTION COVERS THE RIGHT TIME AND PLACE. Go to the page for the individual census database and look for background information. You might learn the collection doesn't contain all extant census schedules, or that the place where your ancestor lived wasn't indexed or wasn't included in that enumeration.

TRY DIFFERENT APPROACHES. Start by entering all you know about the person. If you don't get results, search on fewer terms and combinations of terms.

SEEK ALTERNATE NAME SPELLINGS. A census taker or an indexer might've interpreted the name so outlandishly that a "sounds like" search wouldn't pick up on the misspelling.

LEAVE OUT THE NAME. Instead of a name, search on variables such as residence, birth date and place, place of origin and immigration date.

BE FLEXIBLE. Your ancestor might've lived in a place you didn't expect, or he might have reported a different age or birthplace from the one you were looking for. Use date ranges and try leaving some fields blank to account for uncertainty.

BROWSE. Navigate to schedules for the census year and the enumeration district (ED) where you think your ancestor lived (you can use the ED tools at **<www.stevemorse.org>** to determine the enumeration district). Then, examine the records page by page.

QUESTIONS IN THE CENSUS

▷ **Name**
- **HEAD OF HOUSEHOLD:** 1790, 1800, 1810, 1820, 1830, 1840
- **EVERYONE IN THE HOUSEHOLD (EXCEPT SLAVES):** from 1850 on

▷ **Birth Date and Place**
- **AGE RANGE OF FREE WHITE MALES (RANGES DIFFER):**
  1790, 1800, 1810, 1820, 1830, 1840
- **AGE RANGE OF FREE WHITE FEMALES (RANGES DIFFER):**
  1800, 1810, 1820, 1830, 1840
- **AGE OF EVERYONE IN THE HOUSEHOLD:** 1850 on
- **BIRTHPLACE:** 1850 on
- **BORN WITHIN THE CENSUS YEAR (WITH MONTH):**
  1870, 1880
- **MONTH AND YEAR OF BIRTH:** 1900

▷ Parents
- **FOREIGN-BORN PARENTS:** 1870
- **PARENTS' PLACE OF BIRTH:** 1880 on
- **MOTHER TONGUE:** 1910
- **SELF AND PARENTS' MOTHER TONGUE:** 1920, 1930

▷ Marriage
- **MARRIED WITHIN THE CENSUS YEAR:** 1850, 1860, 1870 (includes the month), 1880, 1890
- **MARITAL STATUS:** 1880 on
- **NUMBER OF YEARS MARRIED:** 1900, 1910
- **AGE AT FIRST MARRIAGE:** 1930

▷ Immigration and Citizenship
- **NUMBER OF ALIENS/PERSONS NOT NATURALIZED:** 1820, 1830, 1840
- **YEAR OF IMMIGRATION TO UNITED STATES:** 1900, 1910, 1920, 1930
- **NUMBER OF YEARS IN UNITED STATES:** 1890, 1900
- **NATURALIZATION STATUS:** 1870 (for males over 21), 1890, 1900, 1910, 1920, 1930

▷ Physical or Mental Health
- **PERSONS IN HOUSEHOLD WHO WERE BLIND, DEAF OR DUMB:** 1830, 1840, 1850, 1860, 1870, 1880, 1890, 1910
- **PERSONS IN HOUSEHOLD WHO WERE IDIOTIC OR INSANE:** 1850, 1860
- **MOTHER OF HOW MANY CHILDREN/NUMBER LIVING:** 1890, 1900, 1910
- **WHETHER SUFFERING FROM CHRONIC DISEASE:** 1890

▷ Personal Property
- **VALUE OF REAL ESTATE OWNED:** 1850, 1860, 1870
- **VALUE OF PERSONAL ESTATE:** 1860, 1870
- **OWN OR RENT HOME:** 1900, 1910, 1920, 1930
- **HAD A RADIO:** 1930

▷ **Education/Occupation**
- **NUMBER OF PERSONS (INCLUDING SLAVES) ENGAGED IN AGRICULTURE, COMMERCE OR MANUFACTURING:** 1820
- **OCCUPATION:** 1840 on
- **ATTENDED SCHOOL IN THE PAST YEAR:** 1840 on
- **CAN READ OR WRITE:** 1850 on

▷ **Other**
- **NUMBER OF FREE COLORED:** 1820, 1830, 1840
- **COLOR/RACE:** 1850 on
- **RELATIONSHIP TO HEAD OF HOUSEHOLD:** 1880 on
- **ABLE TO SPEAK ENGLISH:** 1900, 1910, 1920, 1930
- **VETERAN STATUS:** 1890, 1910 (Civil War only), 1930
- **PENSIONER FOR REVOLUTIONARY OR MILITARY SERVICE:** 1840
- **IF PERSON IS A PAUPER, CONVICT OR HOMELESS CHILD:** 1850, 1860, 1890

NON-POPULATION CENSUSES

SCHEDULES OF DEFECTIVE, DEPENDENT AND DELINQUENT CLASSES : 1880

AGRICULTURAL CENSUSES: 1850, 1860, 1870, 1880

MANUFACTURING AND INDUSTRY SCHEDULES: 1810, 1820, 1850, 1860, 1870, 1880

SLAVE SCHEDULES: 1850, 1860

MORTALITY SCHEDULES: 1850, 1860, 1870, 1880, 1885 (some areas), 1900 (Minnesota only)

US STATE/TERRITORIAL CENSUS: 1885 (some areas)

SOCIAL STATISTICS SCHEDULES: 1850, 1860, 1870, 1885

INDIAN SCHEDULES: 1880, 1900, 1910

INDIAN RESERVATION CENSUSES: 1885 to 1940

INDIAN SCHOOL CENSUSES: 1910 to 1939

REVOLUTIONARY WAR PENSIONERS: 1840

CIVIL WAR VETERANS SCHEDULES: 1890 (extant for half of Kentucky and states alphabetically following)

SCHEDULES OF MILITARY PERSONNEL ON BASES AND VESSELS (INCLUDING OVERSEAS): 1900, 1910, 1920

SCHEDULES OF MERCHANT SEAMEN ON VESSELS: 1930

OFFICIAL CENSUS DATES

1790: August 2
1800: August 4
1810: August 6
1820: August 7
1830-1880: June 1
1890: June 2
1900: June 1
1910: April 15
1920: January 1
1930-2010: April 1

THE SOUNDEX KEY

SOUNDEX CODE	LETTERS
1	b f p v
2	c g j k q s x z
3	d t
4	l
5	m n
6	r
no code	a e h i o u w y

The Soundex indexing system uses a four-character code to help you find similar-sounding surnames in US census records. The code for a surname consists of the first letter of the name plus three numbers representing consonants. Use the following steps to code your ancestors' names.

1. Write the surname. Excepting the first letter, cross out any vowels and the letters *h*, *y* and *w*.

2. Use the first letter of the name as the first letter of your four-character code.

3. Match each subsequent consonant with the corresponding code from the key above until you have three numbers. Ignore the rest of the letters. If adjacent letters have the same number, ignore the second letter. If you run out of letters before your code has three numbers, complete the code with zeros.

WASHINGTON: W252 (coding W-s-n-g)

LEE: L000 (coding the L)

GUTIERREZ: G362 (coding G-t-r-z)

PFISTER: P236 (coding P-s-t-r)

DOBUSH: D120 (coding D-b-s)

THE LOST RULE OF SOUNDEX

A Soundex code determined using the "lost rule" (also known as the H and W Rule) may yield better search results for surnames having an *h* or *w* between two letters of the same code number. Such instances exist in names with combinations such as *thd* or *tht* (such as Rothdeutsch and Smithton), *chs* (Sachse, Ochs), *chk* (Wichkoski) and *schk* (Mitschke, Peschke).

When you formulate a Soundex code in such cases, disregard the *h* or *w* and push the like-coded letters together. For example, *chs* or *schk* would be coded as a single 2, not 22. These examples show the use of the lost rule:

ASHCROFT: A261 (coding A-sc-r-f)

MITSCHKE: M320 (coding M-t-sck-0)

ROTHDEUTSCH: R332 (coding R-td-t-sc)

SCHSEKOWESKE: S220 (coding Scs-k-sk-0)

SOCHSE OR SACHSE: S200 (coding S-cs-0-0)

SMITHTON: S535 (coding S-m-tt-n)

CENSUS ABBREVIATIONS

▷ **Relationships**
A aunt
AD adopted
ADCL adopted child
ADD adopted daughter
ADGCL adopted grandchild
ADM adopted mother
ADS adopted son
BO boarder
B brother
BL or **BIL** brother-in-law
C cousin
D daughter
DL or **DIL** daughter-in-law
F father
FL or **FIL** father-in-law
GF grandfather
GM grandmother
GUA guardian
H husband
L lodger
ML or **MIL** mother-in-law
R roomer
S son
SF stepfather
SM stepmother
SI sister
SL son-in-law
SS stepson
TEN tenant
U uncle
VI visitor
W wife

▷ **Citizenship Status**
AL alien (not naturalized)
PA declaration of intent filed
NA naturalized
NR not recorded

▷ **Color/Ethnicity**
¼ quadroon
⅛ octoroon
W white
B black
CH Chinese
M or **MU** Mulatto
IN Indian
JP Japanese
OT other

▷ **Occupations**
AP apprentice
AT attendant
ASST assistant
BU butler
CAP captain
CHA chamber maid
DLA day laborer
DOM domestic
EMP employee
EN engineer
FAH farm hand
FAL farm laborer
FAW farm worker
GO governess
H.GI hired girl

H.H hired hand
HK housekeeper
H.MAID housemaid
LA laborer
LAU laundry
MAN manager
NU nurse
PH doctor
SA sailor
SE servant
WA warden
WKM workman
WT waiter

▷ **Military**
UA Survivor of the Union Army
UN Survivor of the Union Navy
CA Survivor of the Confederate Army
CN Survivor of the Confederate Navy

IMMIGRATION

US IMMIGRANTS BY COUNTRY
(1820 TO 1975)

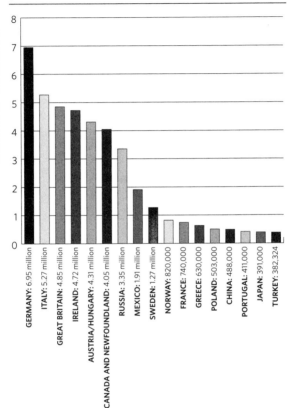

GERMANY: 6.95 million
ITALY: 5.27 million
GREAT BRITAIN: 4.85 million
IRELAND: 4.72 million
AUSTRIA/HUNGARY: 4.31 million
CANADA AND NEWFOUNDLAND: 4.05 million
RUSSIA: 3.35 million
MEXICO: 1.91 million
SWEDEN: 1.27 million
NORWAY: 820,000
FRANCE: 740,000
GREECE: 630,000
POLAND: 503,000
CHINA: 488,000
PORTUGAL: 411,000
JAPAN: 391,000
TURKEY: 382,324

TIMELINE OF IMMIGRATION LAWS

1790 US establishes uniform naturalization rules for white males 21 and older; children of naturalized citizens get automatic citizenship.

1795 Free white females age 21 and older can become citizens.

1804 Widows and children can become citizens if the husband or father died before filing final papers.

1824 Alien minors, upon turning 21, can be naturalized if they've lived in the United States for five years.

1855 Alien women become citizens upon marrying US citizens.

1862 Aliens who've received honorable discharges from the US Army can skip filing declarations of intention.

1868 14th Amendment declares former slaves citizens.

1870 People of African descent may become citizens.

1882 Chinese Exclusion Act passes.

1887 Dawes Act entitles American Indians who've accepted land allotments to become citizens.

1891 Bureau of Immigration is established.

1894 Declaration of intention waived for aliens who are honorably discharged after five years in the Navy or Marine Corps.

1906 Bureau of Immigration and Naturalization Service (INS) is established.

1917 Puerto Ricans become US citizens.

1922 Married women's citizenship becomes independent of their husbands'.

1924 American Indians are granted full citizenship; quotas severely reduce immigration.

1929 Photographs are required on petition for naturalization.

1940 Alien Registration Act required non-naturalized aliens to register with the government.

1943 Asian immigrants can become citizens.

1952 Age requirement for naturalization drops to 18; declaration of intention becomes optional.

1990 Courts no longer naturalize citizens.

2003 INS becomes US Citizenship and Immigration Services.

PASSENGER LIST AVAILABILITY FOR BUSIEST US PORTS

PASSENGER LIST	AVAILIBILITY
BALTIMORE	1820-1897, 1891-1957
BEAUFORT, NC	1865
BOSTON	1820-1874, 1883-1891, 1891-1943
BRIDGEPORT, CONN.	1870, 1929-1959

PASSENGER LIST	AVAILIBILITY
CHARLESTON, SC	1820-1829, 1865, 1890-1939
GALVESTON, TEXAS	1846-1951
GLOUCESTER, MASS.	1820, 1832-1839, 1867-1868, 1870, 1906-1943
GULFPORT AND PASCAGOULA, MISS.	1903-1954
KEY WEST, FLA.	1837-1852, 1857-1868, 1890-1945
NEW BEDFORD, MASS.	1822, 1825-1852, 1902-1954
NEW LONDON, CONN.	1820-1847, 1929-1959
NEW ORLEANS	1813-1952
NEWPORT, RI	1820-1852, 1857
NEW YORK CITY	1789-1957
NORFOLK AND PORTSMOUTH, VA.	1820-1857
PENSACOLA, FLA.	1890-1948
PHILADELPHIA	1800-1882, 1883-1948
PORTLAND, MAINE	1893-1943
PROVIDENCE, RI	1820-1867, 1911-1954
SAN FRANCISCO	1882-1957
SAVANNAH, GA.	1820-1826, 1831, 1847-1851, 1865-1868, 1890-1945
SEATTLE	1882-1957
WILMINGTON, DEL.	1820, 1830-1831, 1833, 1840-1849
US-CANADA BORDER	1895 to 1956
US-MEXICO BORDER	1903-1950s

LOOK FOR CLUES IN CENSUS RECORDS. US censuses from 1900 to 1930 give the year of immigration and indicate whether someone is naturalized. Many censuses also provide a birthplace (usually a country).

TRY TO FIND OUT THE PERSON'S NAME AT BIRTH, which is how he'll probably appear on passenger lists. Many immigrants changed their names after arrival to sound more "American."

SEARCH FOR ALTERNATE NAME SPELLINGS. The name may have been mistranscribed or misindexed, your ancestor may have altered the spelling, or the ship's clerk may have written it down incorrectly.

SEARCH IMMIGRATION AND EMIGRATION COLLECTIONS on websites such as Ancestry.com **<ancestry.com>** (by subscription), the National Archives' Access to Archival Databases **<aad.archives.gov>**, Ellis Island **<elilsisland.org>**, Castle Garden **<castlegarden.org>**, the FamilySearch Record Search Pilot **<pilot.familysearch.org>**, Information Wanted **<infowanted.bc.edu>**, and the Immigrant Ships Transcribers' Guild **<immigrantships.net>**.

SEARCH FOR WOMEN UNDER BOTH THEIR MAIDEN AND MARRIED NAMES. If you can't find a mother, look for her children.

SEARCH FOR YOUR ANCESTOR'S NEIGHBORS AND FRIENDS on passenger lists, since many immigrants traveled and settled with those from their hometowns.

BROWSE PASSENGER RECORDS for the arrival date or year using an online collection or a tool such Steve Morse's One-Step search site **<stevemorse.org>**.

IMMIGRATION

CHECK NATURALIZATION RECORDS for an immigrant's birth name. These records are available through the USCIS Genealogy Service **<www.uscis.gov/genealogy>** (see the next page) for 1906 and later years; records for various years and locales are available on subscription sites Ancestry.com and Footnote **<footnote.com>**, and on microfilm you can rent from the Family History Library **<www.familysearch.org>**.

PASSENGER LIST NOTATIONS AND ABBREVIATIONS

ADMITTED: passenger allowed to enter the United States

C or **NAT** followed by numbers: passenger's naturalization certificate file number

C/A: certificate of arrival

DEPORTED: passenger refused entry and returned home

DCD: discharged

IN HOSPITAL: immigrant was hospitalized for illness; an outcome may note the passenger was discharged, deported or died in the hospital

LPC: likely public charge

NAME LINED OUT: passenger's name was changed or corrected; the corrected name is written in

NOB, NOT SHIPPED or **PASSENGER'S ENTRY LINED OUT:** not on board; passenger didn't board the ship or was re-recorded elsewhere on the list (may be due to an incorrectly recorded cabin class)

SI: passenger was referred to the Board of Special Inquiry for further evaluation

TRANSIT: passenger was en route to another country or did not plan to stay in the United States

USB: US-born

USC: US citizen

X, **D** or **HELD:** passenger was detained at the port of entry

RECORDS AVAILABLE THROUGH THE USCIS GENEALOGY SERVICE

NATURALIZATION CERTIFICATE FILES (C-FILES):
Sept. 27, 1906 to March 31, 1956

ALIEN REGISTRATION FORM (FORM AR-2):
August 1940 to March 1944

VISA FILES: July 1, 1924 to March 31, 1944

REGISTRY FILES: March 1929 to March 31, 1944

IMMIGRANT FILES (A-FILES): April 1, 1944 to May 1, 1951

MILITARY

TIMELINE OF US MILITARY CONFLICTS

MILITARY

1622-1644 POWHATAN WARS: Jamestown settlers and Powhatan Indians clash.

1637 PEQUOT WAR: Pequot Indians and Puritan settlers battle in the Connecticut River Valley.

1675-1676 KING PHILIP'S WAR: Indian leader Metacomet (aka King Philip) organizes New England tribes in a revolt against Colonial expansion.

1676 BACON'S REBELLION: Nathaniel Bacon leads unauthorized expeditions against Indians.

1677-1679 CULPEPER'S REBELLION: Albemarle, Carolina colonists imprison the deputy governor, convene a legislature and run the government.

1689-1697 KING WILLIAM'S WAR: The French and Indians attack British in New York, New Hampshire and Maine.

1689-1691 LEISLER'S REBELLION: Militia captain Jacob Leisler names himself governor of New York and tries to organize an expedition against French Canada.

1702-1713 QUEEN ANNE'S WAR: French and Indians attack British settlements; British capture Acadia.

1711-1713 TUSCARORA WAR: Tuscarora Indians attack settlers along North Carolina's Neuse and Pamlico rivers.

1715-1716 YAMASEE WAR: Creek, Yamasee, Apalachee, Savannah and Sarraw Indians attack South Carolina settlements.

1739-1742 WAR OF JENKINS' EAR: England declares war on Spain as both nations try to expand their interests in America.

1744-1748 KING GEORGE'S WAR: French, Indians and Spanish fight the British from French Canada to the Caribbean.

1754-1763 FRENCH AND INDIAN WAR: British regulars and American colonials square off against the French and their Indian allies. The capture of Quebec ends French rule in Canada.

1760-1762 CHEROKEE UPRISING: British and Cherokee fight in Tennessee, Virginia and the Carolinas.

1763-1766 PONTIAC'S WAR: Pontiac leads the Ottawa, Wyandot, Potawatomi and Ojibwa in an attempt to drive British settlers out of former French territories.

1763-1764 PAXTON BOYS UPRISING: Pennsylvania frontiersmen march on Philadelphia and raid the Conestoga Indians.

1765-1766 STAMP ACT REVOLT: Sons of Liberty resist Britain's Stamp Act; it's repealed in March 1766.

1768-1771 REGULATOR WAR: Western North Carolina colonists fight government officials.

1770 BOSTON MASSACRE: British soldiers kill five Bostonians.

1773 BOSTON TEA PARTY: Colonists dressed as Indians board ships and dump tea into Boston Harbor.

1774 LORD DUNMORE'S WAR: Shawnee Indians fight Virginia settlers over colonists' expansion into the Appalachians.

1775-1783 AMERICAN REVOLUTION: Colonies fight for independence from Great Britain.

1786-1787 SHAYS' REBELLION: Suffering from a harsh economy, Massachusetts farmers march on Springfield; the state militia defeats the uprising.

1790-1812 OHIO VALLEY CAMPAIGNS: US forces fight sporadic battles with Miami, Shawnee and other tribes in what's now Ohio, Indiana and Illinois.

1794 WHISKEY REBELLION: Western Pennsylvanians protest the government's new tax on whiskey.

1798-1800 QUASI-WAR WITH FRANCE: French privateers prey on US merchant vessels, prompting an undeclared naval war between the United States and France.

1801-1805 FIRST BARBARY WAR: The United States attacks the Barbary state of Tripoli after refusing to pay tribute to pirates.

1812-1815 WAR OF 1812: The United States takes on British forces, who burn Washington, DC.

1815 SECOND BARBARY WAR: Algiers declares war on the United States.

1817-1818 FIRST SEMINOLE WAR: Conflict begins after US authorities try to reclaim runaway slaves living among the Seminole.

1832 BLACK HAWK WAR: Illinois and Wisconsin militia, supported by the US Army, take on the Sauk, Fox, Winnebago, Sioux and Chippewa tribes.

1835-1842 SECOND SEMINOLE WAR: War erupts after the Seminole Indians refuse to relocate west of the Mississippi River.

1836 WAR OF TEXAS INDEPENDENCE: American settlers in Texas fight Mexico for independence.

1838-1839 TRAIL OF TEARS: US soldiers relocate Cherokee Indians from eastern states to Oklahoma Territory. More than 4,000 Cherokee die during the journey.

1838-1839 AROOSTOOK WAR: Maine farmers and Canadian lumbermen clash over border territory.

1839-1846 ANTI-RENT WAR: New York farmers rebel against feudal landowner system.

1842 DORR REBELLION: An attempt to reform Rhode Island's 1663 charter, under which only landowners can vote, becomes an armed uprising.

1846-1848 MEXICAN WAR: Mexico cedes what's now California, New Mexico, Arizona, Colorado, Utah and Nevada to the United States.

1855-1858 THIRD SEMINOLE WAR: The Seminole are defeated and moved from Florida.

1857-1858 UTAH WAR: President Buchanan sends troops to enforce his appointment of non-Mormon governor Alfred Cumming.

1860-1900 PLAINS AND WESTERN INDIAN WARS: Western states witness repeated conflicts between US settlers and American Indian inhabitants.

1861-1865 CIVIL WAR: Southern and Northern states fight over slavery and states' rights issues.

1864-1868 NAVAJO WARS: After a series of treaties fails, Col. Kit Carson begins a scorched-earth policy that forces the Indians to surrender.

1866-1871 THE FENIAN WAR: Irish-American movement launches five unsuccessful raids in Canada.

1898 SPANISH-AMERICAN WAR: United States declares war on Spain and launches offensives in Cuba and the Philippines.

1899-1902 PHILIPPINE INSURRECTION: US troops clash with Filipino freedom fighters.

1900 BOXER REBELLION: United States is part of an international force that ends a siege of Beijing.

1898-1934 THE BANANA WARS: Marines quell revolts in Haiti, the Dominican Republic, Nicaragua, Panama and Cuba.

1916-1917 PANCHO VILLA EXPEDITION: US troops pursue the bandit and revolutionary Pancho Villa in Mexico.

1917-1918 WORLD WAR I: More than 4 million Americans serve in the "The Great War."

1919-1920 RUSSIAN REVOLUTION: The United States deploys to Vladivostok and Siberia to support anti-Bolshevik forces.

1941-1945 WORLD WAR II: More than 16 million Americans fight in Europe, North Africa and the Pacific.

1950-1953 KOREAN WAR: US troops, supported by the United Nations, help South Korea fight off invasions from North Korea in this military conflict, which was the first significant armed conflict of the Cold War.

EARLY 1960s-1973 VIETNAM WAR: US troops aid South Vietnam against communist North Vietnam and its Viet Cong allies in this Cold War conflict.

WAR RECORDS TO SEARCH FOR

Learn which military records to search for based on your ancestors' birth dates.

IF AN ANCESTOR WAS BORN IN ...	LOOK FOR RECORDS OF THE ...
1726-1767	Revolutionary War (1775-1783)
1762-1799	War of 1812 (1812-1815)
1796-1831	Mexican War (1846-1848)
1811-1848	Civil War (1861-1865)
1848-1881	Spanish-American War (1898)
1849-1885	Philippine Insurrection (1899-1902)
1872-1900	World War I (1917-1918)
1877-1925	World War II (1941-1945)
1900-1936	Korean War (1950-1953)
1914-1955	Vietnam War (early 1960s-1973)

MAJOR GENEALOGICAL RECORDS
GENERATED FROM US WARS

Depending on the war in which your ancestor served, you'll find a variety of types of military records.

WAR	SERVICE RECORDS/ MUSTER ROLLS	PENSION RECORDS	BOUNTY-LAND WARRANTS	DRAFT CARDS
Colonial Wars	X		X	
Revolutionary War	X	X	X	
War of 1812	X	X	X	
Mexican War	X	X	X	
Civil War	X	X		
Spanish American War	X			
World War I	X			X
World War II	X			X
Korean War	X			
Vietnam War	X			

WHERE TO LOOK
FOR US MILITARY RECORDS

Check the repositories and websites listed for original military records on paper, on microfilm, or in digitized format. Large public, state and university libraries also may have copies of NARA microfilm; search for books and websites with military record indexes and transcriptions, too.

REVOLUTIONARY WAR SERVICE RECORDS
- Ancestry.com **<ancestry.com>** (by subscription)
- Footnote **<footnote.com>** (by subscription)

REVOLUTIONARY WAR PENSION FILES
- Footnote
- HeritageQuest Online (available through subscribing libraries)
- NARA and Family History Library microfilm

CIVIL WAR SERVICE RECORDS
- Footnote
- NARA

CIVIL WAR US COLORED TROOPS SERVICE RECORDS
- Ancestry.com
- NARA and Family History Library microfilm

CIVIL WAR PENSION INDEX CARDS
- Ancestry.com: extends to 1934
- FamilySearch Record Search (index only)
- Footnote
- NARA and Family History Library microfilm

CIVIL WAR PENSIONS
• NARA

CIVIL WAR WIDOWS' PENSION FILES
• Footnote

MEXICAN WAR SERVICE AND PENSION RECORDS
• NARA

SPANISH-AMERICAN WAR SERVICE RECORDS
• NARA

WWI DRAFT REGISTRATION CARDS
• Ancestry.com
• NARA and Family History Library microfilm

WWI AND LATER SERVICE RECORDS
• NARA (restricted for privacy reasons)

WWII DRAFT REGISTRATION CARDS
• Ancestry.com
• FamilySearch Record Search
• NARA and Family History Library microfilm

WWII ENLISTMENT DATABASE
• Ancestry.com
• Footnote
• NARA website **<archives.gov>**

ROSTERS, MUSTER ROLLS, MILITIA RECORDS, ADJUTANT GENERAL RECORDS, VETERANS SURVEYS, CORRESPONDENCE, PHOTOS, BATTLEFIELD MAPS, REGIMENTAL HISTORIES
• State archives
• Military history organizations

MILITARY HISTORY ORGANIZATIONS

AIR FORCE HISTORICAL RESEARCH AGENCY
600 Chennault Circle, Building 1405,
Maxwell Air Force Base, AL 36112,
(334) 953-2395, **<www.afhra.af.mil>**

CIVIL WAR PRESERVATION TRUST
1156 15th St. NW, Suite 900, Washington, DC 20005
(202) 367-1861, **<civilwar.org>**

CONFEDERATE RESEARCH CENTER
Box 619, Hillsboro, TX 76645, (254) 582-2555,
<www.hillcollege.edu/info/texasheritagemuseum>

DAUGHTERS OF UNION VETERANS OF THE CIVIL WAR
503 S. Walnut St., Springfield, IL 62704, (217) 544-0616,
<www.duvcw.org>

DESCENDANTS OF MEXICAN WAR VETERANS
Box 830482, Richardson, TX 75083, **<www.dmwv.org>**

GRAND ARMY OF THE REPUBLIC MUSEUM AND LIBRARY
4278 Griscom St., Philadelphia, PA 19124,
(215) 289-6484, **<garmuslib.org>**

NATIONAL MUSEUM OF THE MARINE CORPS
Box 998, Quantico, VA 22134, (800) 397-7585,
<www.usmcmuseum.org>

**NATIONAL SOCIETY DAUGHTERS
OF THE AMERICAN REVOLUTION**
1776 D St. NW, Washington, DC 20006,
(202) 628-1776, **<www.dar.org>**

NAVAL HISTORICAL CENTER
Washington Navy Yard, 805 Kidder Breese St. SE,
Washington, DC 20374, (202) 433-3224,
<www.history.navy.mil>

SONS OF THE AMERICAN REVOLUTION
1000 S. Fourth St., Louisville, KY 40203,
(502) 589-1776, **<www.sar.org>**

SONS OF CONFEDERATE VETERANS
Box 59, Columbia, TN 38402, (800) 693-4943, **<scv.org>**

SONS OF UNION VETERANS OF THE CIVIL WAR
Box 1865, Harrisburg, PA 17105, (717) 232-7000,
<www.suvcw.org>

UNITED DAUGHTERS OF THE CONFEDERACY
328 North Blvd., Richmond, VA 23220,
(804) 355-1636, **<www.hqudc.org>**

US ARMY CENTER OF MILITARY HISTORY
Collins Hall, 103 Third Ave., Fort Lesley J. McNair,
Washington, DC 20319, (202) 685-4042,
<www.history.army.mil>

US ARMY MILITARY HISTORY INSTITUTE
ARMY HERITAGE AND EDUCATION CENTER
950 Soldiers Drive, Carlisle, PA 17013,
(717) 245-3971, **<www.carlisle.army.mil/ahec>**

CEMETERIES

TOMBSTONE SYMBOLISM

▷ **Architectural**
ARCHWAY, DOOR OR GATE: passageway into the next life

BENCH: places of contemplation for mourners

PILLAR OR COLUMN, BROKEN: life cut short or sudden death

▷ **Animals**
BAT: death; misfortune

CRANE: loyalty, vigilance

DOVE: peace

LAMB: meekness, gentleness, innocence; God's flock; popular on children's graves

LION: courage, strength, resurrection

PHOENIX: resurrection

▷ **Clothing**
HELMET: protection, faith

SHOES, EMPTY, ONE OVERTURNED: loss of a child

▷ **Figures**
ANGEL, DROPPING FLOWERS ON GRAVE: grief, mourning

ANGEL, POINTING TO HEAVEN: rejoicing

BABY OR CHILD, NAKED: new life, innocence, purity

HEAD WITH WINGS: soul effigy indicating human mortality

▷ Fruits, Nuts and the Harvest
ACORN: strength, independence

FRUIT: eternal plenty

PINEAPPLE: welcome, perfection

WHEAT: harvest, prosperity; deceased full of years

▷ Hands and Fingers
COHANIM HANDS (thumbs and forefingers touch)**:** Judaism

FOREFINGER POINTING UP: soul has gone to heaven

HAND, REACHING DOWN: God retrieving the deceased's soul

HANDSHAKE: God's welcome into heaven; marriage, if one hand is feminine and the other, masculine

▷ Initials
AAONMS: Ancient Arabic Order or Nobles and the Mystic Shrine (Masonic)

AASR: Ancient and Accepted Scottish Rite (Masonic)

AOH: Ancient Order of Hibernians

AOUW: Ancient Order of United Workmen

BPOE: Benevolent and Protective Order of Elks

FOE: Fraternal Order of Eagles

G (with a compass and square)**:** Masonic

IHC, HIS: the first three letters of Jesus' name in Greek

IOOF: Independent Order of Odd Fellows

K OF C: Knights of Columbus

WOW: Woodmen of the World

▷ **Mortality**
BONE: death

CANDLE: life

CLOCK: the march of time, usually stopped at the hour of death

SKULL, WITH CROSSBONES OR WINGS: version of the winged death's head symbolizing the fleeting nature of life

▷ **Occupations and Crafts**
CHURCH WITH A STEEPLE: minister

HORSES, TWO HEADS: International Brotherhood of Teamsters, Chauffeurs, Warehousemen and Helpers of America

SCALES OF JUSTICE: lawyer

SHIP: sailor or fisherman

▷ **Ornamental**
BASKET: maternal body, fertility

CROOK: associated with Jesus as a shepherd; often on the graves of Odd Fellows

DRAPED URN: physical body; veil may refer to reverence or a veil between earth and heaven

FOUNTAIN: the Virgin Mary

SHIELD: protection; faith; defense of the spirit

▷ **Religious**
CROSS: Christianity

STAR OF DAVID, MENORAH, LEVITE PITCHER, COHANIM HANDS
(see Hands and Fingers) : Judaism

▷ **Trees, Plants and Flowers**
DAISY: simplicity, the Virgin Mary; often on the graves of children

FERN: humility, sincerity

LILY: purity

MORNING GLORY: resurrection

OAK LEAF: strength of faith

OLIVE TREE OR BRANCH: reconciliation between God and man; peace

THISTLE: Scottish heritage

TREE STUMP: life cut short, often on graves of members of Woodmen of the World

VINE: relationship between God and man

WHEAT: long, fruitful life

WEEPING WILLOW, SOMETIMES WITH URN: sorrow

CEMETERY RESEARCH DOS AND DON'TS

▷ **Do ...**

• bring a camera, reflective surface (such as foil-covered cardboard), notebook, pens, carpenter's apron, gardener's knee pads, garden shears, whisk broom, sunscreen and moist towelettes.

• wear protective clothing and boots and carry bug repellent.

• take personal safety precautions, such as bringing a friend and carrying your cell phone.

• watch for uneven ground, since graves tend to sink.

• notice who's buried around your ancestor—they could be relatives.

• note the exact location in relationship to the cemetery entrance (record the GPS coordinates if you have a device) and mark it on a cemetery map.

• take pictures of the tombstone with a variety of lighting and angles. Also photograph the grounds and graveyard entrance.

• note the type of stone that marks your ancestor's grave and and any artwork on the stone

• write down the full inscription on the stone.

• bring rubbing wax or jumbo crayons, scissors, a helper and nonfusible, medium to heavyweight interfacing fabric to do a tombstone rubbing—but only if the stone is stable and in good shape.

- get permission do a tombstone rubbing. (In some states, such as Massachusetts, it's illegal.)

- when you get a tombstone rubbing home, iron it face up and covered with an old towel.

- leave flowers with your contact information attached on or shortly before Memorial Day or the town's decoration day—a distant cousin might show up to pay respects.

▷ **Don't ...**
- just rush to find your ancestor's grave, photograph the tombstone and leave.

- visit when it's getting dark, or go alone to an isolated cemetery.

- cross private land to get to a cemetery, unless you get the landowner's permission first.

- clean or otherwise touch any tombstones that are crumbling or unstable.

- use acidic compounds such as vinegar or shaving cream on tombstones—they can eat away at the stone.

- use chalk on tombstones (it leaves a residue).

- get any wax or crayon on the tombstone when you do a rubbing.

- do a tombstone rubbing where it's against laws or cemetery rules.

- interfere with anyone paying respects or attending funerals.

TOMBSTONE MATERIALS TIMELINE

1650s AND EARLIER: fieldstones, boulders and wood markers

1660s–1850s: sandstone, limestone and slate

1830s–1880s: marble

1880s–1910s: soft, gray granite and cast metal

1920s–PRESENT: granite

TYPES OF CEMETERIES

CHURCH/RELIGIOUS: May be adjacent to a church or other religious organization's building; especially common in New England and the Southeast.

ETHNIC: A cemetery where those of a particular ethnicity were historically buried. May also be a religious or other type of cemetery.

FAMILY or **PRIVATE:** Small plots with graves of local families often in a rural setting; usually maintained by the town or county government or a local historical society.

GARDEN: Beautifully landscaped with trees, flowers, fountains and paths winding around monuments and tombstones; popular starting in the 1800s.

MEMORIAL PARK: Landscaped lawns and gardens with flat, ground-level plaques marking graves; introduced starting in the early 1900s.

POTTER'S FIELDS: Public cemeteries where the poor and unclaimed bodies often were buried.

VETERANS CEMETERIES: Nationally, state or locally owned military cemeteries where veterans and their families may be buried.

4 CEMETERY SEARCH TIPS

1. FIND THE BURIAL PLACE. Try to learn where your ancestor is buried from funeral cards, death certificates, obituaries or other family papers. If these sources list a funeral home, check the *American Blue Book of Funeral Service* (Kates-Boylston Publications) for contact information. If the home no longer exists, run a Google **<google.com>** search to see if another home bought it, and check local or state historical societies for information on what happened to its records.

2. LOOK FOR PUBLISHED TOMBSTONE TRANSCRIPTIONS. Before you travel to a distant cemetery, look for a published transcription. Search the Family History Library's (FHL) online catalog **<www.familysearch.org>** on the place name, then look for a cemetery category in your results. You can rent FHL microfilm through your local branch Family History Center. On many websites (see Cemetery Research Resources), you can search volunteer-submitted tombstone transcriptions and photographs.

3. GET BURIAL RECORDS. Many transcriptions are online, posted by fellow genealogists, cemeteries or government agencies. Search the sites in the next section. If the record isn't online, write to the cemetery sexton if the cemetery is still active. For inactive cemeteries, write to the town hall or county courthouse where the cemetery is located.

4. CHECK VITAL STATS. Some tombstone markers offer just a name and death date. More-elaborate stones may give the date of birth, places of birth and death, age at death, parents' and spouse's names, and a verse (called the epitaph). You may see a person's age written this way: "Died March 25, 1846, aged 37 years, 3 months and 15 days." To determine the birth date, you can use an online calculator such as the one at **<www.longislandgenealogy.com/birth.html>**.

CEMETERY RESEARCH RESOURCES

▷ **Websites**
THE A TO Z OF TOMBSTONE ART
<www.tales.co.uk/index-atozart.html>

AMERICAN BATTLE MONUMENTS COMMISSION
<www.abmc.gov>

CEMETERY JUNCTION
<www.cemeteryjunction.com>

CEMETERY SYMBOLISM: A WARY GLOSSARY
<www.alsirat.com/symbols/symbols1.html>

CYNDI'S LIST: CEMETERIES
<cyndislist.com/cemetery.htm>

FIND A GRAVE
<www.findagrave.com>

GENEALOGY.COM VIRTUAL CEMETERY
<www.genealogy.com/vcem_welcome.html>

INTERMENT.NET
<www.interment.net>

NAMES IN STONE
<namesinstone.com>

NATIONWIDE GRAVESITE LOCATOR
<gravelocator.cem.va.gov>

OBITUARY CENTRAL
<www.obitcentral.com>

SAVING GRAVES
<www.savinggraves.net>

USGENWEB TOMBSTONE TRANSCRIPTION PROJECT
<www.usgwtombstones.org>

USGS GEOGRAPHIC NAMES INFORMATION SYSTEM
<geonames.usgs.gov>: Select Cemetery from the Feature
Class list when you search for known cemeteries in the area.

▷ **Books**
*The American Resting Place: 400 Years of History
Through Our Cemeteries and Burial Grounds*
by Marilyn Yalom (Houghton Mifflin Harcourt)

*Cemeteries of the US: A Guide to Contact
Information for US Cemeteries and Their Records*
by Deborah M. Burek (Gale Group)

Stories in Stone: The Complete Guide to Cemetery Symbolism by
Douglas Keister (Gibbs Smith)

Your Guide to Cemetery Research by Sharon DeBartolo
Carmack (Betterway Books)

3 STEPS TO PHOTOGRAPHING
A TOMBSTONE

1. BRING THE RIGHT TOOLS. To take a photograph of a tombstone, you'll need:

- camera and memory card (or film), plus extra batteries
- spray bottle filled with water
- plastic or nylon brush (never wire)
- rags
- mirror (preferably full-length) or foil-covered cardboard

2. PREP THE TOMBSTONE. If the stone is sturdy and in good shape, lightly clean it by spraying it with water and gently removing debris with your brush and rag.

If the stone is crumbling or unsteady, don't touch it. Wet the stone to bring out the transcription (avoid any other substances such as chalk or shaving cream).

3. GET GOOD LIGHTING. Photographs turn out better when taken in early morning light. In many cemeteries, graves lie on an east-west axis, and late afternoon light may cast your shadow on west-facing inscriptions. Use a mirror or foil to reflect light onto the stone for a better photograph (bring along an assistant to hold the reflector).

GENETIC GENEALOGY

GENETIC GENEALOGY TESTING COMPANIES

23ANDME
<www.23andme.com>

AFRICAN ANCESTRY
<www.africanancestry.com>

AFRICANDNA
<www.africandna.com>

ANCESTRY.COM DNA
<dna.ancestry.com>

DECODEME
<www.decodeme.com>

DNA CONSULTANTS
<dnaconsultants.com>

DNA DIAGNOSTICS CENTER
<www.ancestrybydna.com>

DNA HERITAGE
<dnaheritage.com>

FAMILY TREE DNA
<www.familytreedna.com>

FAMILYBUILDER
<www.familybuilder.com>

GENETREE
<www.genetree.com>

NATIONAL GEORGRAPHIC GENOGRAPHIC PROJECT
<genographic.
nationalgeographic.
com/genographic>

OXFORD ANCESTORS
<www.oxfordancestors.com>

PATHWAY GENOMICS
<www.pathway.com>

DNA TEST RESULTS DATABASES

ANCESTRY.COM DNA
<dna.ancestry.com>: Search the Y-DNA and mtDNA databases free (registration is required).

GENETREE
<www.genetree.com>: This genetic genealogy-meets-social networking site offers mtDNA and Y-DNA tests, and lets you search Sorenson Molecular Genealogy Foundation databases.

MITOSEARCH
<www.mitosearch.org>: This Family Tree DNA database has mtDNA test results.

OMNIPOP
<www.cstl.nist.gov/biotech/strbase/populationdata.htm>: This database has test results from volunteers around the world, useful for comparing DNA profiles, but it's tricky to use. Through the testing company DNA Consultants, you can order an analysis comparing your results to Omnipop.

SORENSON MOLECULAR GENEALOGY FOUNDATION (SMGF)
<www.smgf.org>: Enter Y-DNA or mtDNA marker values or a surname to search the databases of SMGF study participants' results, which are linked to pedigree information. The database also is searchable through the GeneTree website.

YBASE
<www.ybase.org>: Though DNA Heritage runs this site, you can enter up to 49 Y-DNA markers from any lab's results. This site's technical language makes it primarily for the scientific community, but if you're game, click Search by Haplotype or Search by Surname.

YHRD

<www.yhrd.org>: This site also is primarily for the scientific community. To search it, click the Search tab.

YSEARCH

<www.ysearch.org>: Family Tree DNA has created conversion pages to help you upload results from any testing company to this database.

TYPES OF GENETIC GENEALOGY TESTS

TEST	WHAT IT DOES	WHO CAN TAKE IT
Y-DNA	Determines whether families with the same last name are related and estimates when the common ancestor lived. Results relate only to male lineage. Results can determine a haplogroup.	Men (a woman can have her paternal grandfather, father, brother, father's brother or the brother's son take the test)
mitochondrial (mt) DNA	Best for learning about ancient maternal-line ancestry. Can confirm a relationship, but does not estimate when the common ancestor lived. Results assign a haplogroup.	Men and women
ethnic	Compares your DNA markers to those typical of people of certain ethnicities, such as African-Americans or American Indians.	Men and women
biogeographical	Examines autosomal DNA markers to determine genetic heritage (or admixture) among anthropological groups.	Men and women
autosomal (short tandem repeat, or STR)	Can confirm a relationship to a living person, including what relationship (if any) exists. Both individuals must provide a DNA sample.	Men and women

MYTH: Geneticists use hair and blood samples to trace a person's ancestry.
REALITY: Genetic genealogy tests usually involve swishing mouthwash or taking a cheek swab.

MYTH: A DNA test can pinpoint precisely where your ancestors lived or which tribe they belonged to.
REALITY: Human migration throughout history makes pinpointing ancestral locations or tribes extremely difficult. Combining genetic genealogy with traditional research, though, can help you discover ancestral origins.

MYTH: To find out if you and another researcher descend from the same third-great-grandfather, you need to dig up his body for a DNA sample to test.
REALITY: Find a descendant of your third-great-grandfather through a male line, and ask him to take a test. This man would have inherited Great-great-great-grandpa's Y-DNA.

MYTH: The results of ancestral DNA tests are 99.9 percent accurate, just like the DNA tests on CSI.
REALITY: Genetic genealogy involves a lot of analysis and interpretation. DNA test results are presented in terms of probabilities. In most cases, they can suggest—but not prove—relationships.

MYTH: If you take a DNA test, you can finally find out who your great-grandmother's parents were.
REALITY: A DNA test can't identify who your ancestors were.

GENETIC GENEALOGY

You and your male co-worker have the same last name. Are you related?

MAN: Both of you should get your Y-DNA tested and compare the results.

WOMAN: Assuming your maiden name is the one your co-worker shares, ask a male relative with that name (your father or brother, or your father's brother or his son) to get his Y-DNA tested. You'd then compare your male relative's test results to your co-worker's. If your married name is the same as your co-worker's, have your husband take the Y-DNA test.

You and your female co-worker have the same last name. Are you related?

MAN: If your co-worker's maiden name is the same as your last name, you should get your Y-DNA tested, and she should ask a male relative with that last name to get his Y-DNA tested.

WOMAN: If your maiden names are the same, each of you should ask a male relative with that name to test his Y-DNA.

Your mother's maiden name is Wheeler. You want to know if her father was related to other Wheelers in a surname study you heard about.

MAN AND WOMAN: Your grandfather didn't pass down Y-DNA or mtDNA to your mother, so neither she nor you can get tested. If your grandfather's living, he could take a Y-DNA test, which you can compare to results in the study. Your grandfather would've given his Y-DNA to a son, so your mother's brother could take the test. If this uncle had sons (your cousins), they share his Y-DNA and could get tested. Can't find any male relatives who inherited your maternal grandfather's Y-DNA? Climb further up your family tree—see if that grandfather had brothers who had sons, or if his father (your great-grandfather) had brothers who had sons.

According to family lore, you have an American Indian ancestor on your father's maternal line. How can you confirm the story?

MAN AND WOMAN: You'd need to have your father's mtDNA tested—not your own, since your father didn't pass down his mtDNA to you or your siblings. You also could have one of your father's siblings tested, since his mtDNA is identical to theirs. If your father has a sister, she would've passed down that same mtDNA to her children, so they could be tested. And if your father's sister has a daughter, she or any of the daughter's children can be tested.

GENETIC GENEALOGY RESOURCES

▷ **Websites**
10 GREAT BLOGS FOR GENETIC GENEALOGISTS
<www.blogs.com/topten/10-great-blogs-for-genetic-genealogists>

CYNDI'S LIST: GENETICS, DNA AND FAMILY HEALTH
<www.cyndislist.com/dna.htm>

CYNDI'S LIST: SURNAME DNA STUDIES AND PROJECTS
<www.cyndislist.com/surn-dna.htm>

DNA-NEWBIE MAILING LIST
<lists.rootsweb.com/index/other/DNA/DNA-NEWBIE.html>

GENETEALOGY
<www.genetealogy.com>

THE GENETIC GENEALOGIST
<www.thegeneticgenealogist.com>

INTERNATIONAL SOCIETY OF GENETIC GENEALOGY
<isogg.org>

JOURNAL OF GENETIC GENEALOGY
<www.jogg.info>

ROOTS TELEVISION DNA CHANNEL
<www.rootstelevision.com/players/player_dna3.php>

▷ **Books**
Deep Ancestry: Inside The Genographic Project by Spencer Wells (National Geographic)

DNA & Genealogy by Colleen Fitzpatrick (Rice Book Press)

DNA and Tradition: The Genetic Link to the Ancient Hebrews by Yaakov Kleiman (Devora Publishing)

The Seven Daughters of Eve by Bryan Sykes (W.W. Norton & Co.)

Saxons, Vikings, and Celts: The Genetic Roots of Britain and Ireland by Bryan Sykes (W.W. Norton & Co.)

Trace Your Roots With DNA by Megan Smolenyak Smolenyak and Ann Turner (Rodale)

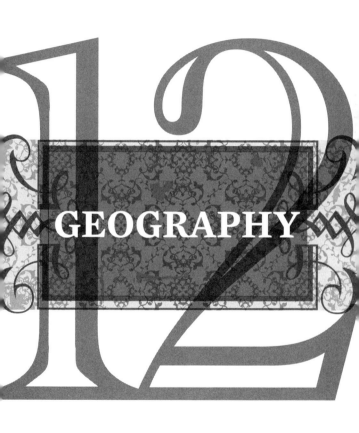

GEOGRAPHY

RECTANGULAR SURVEY SYSTEM

SECTIONS IN A TOWNSHIP

					640 acres
6	5	4	3	2	1
7	8	9	10	11	12
13	14	15	16	17	18
19	20	21	22	23	24
30	29	28	27	26	25
31	32	33	34	35	36

6 miles (vertical) — 6 miles (horizontal)

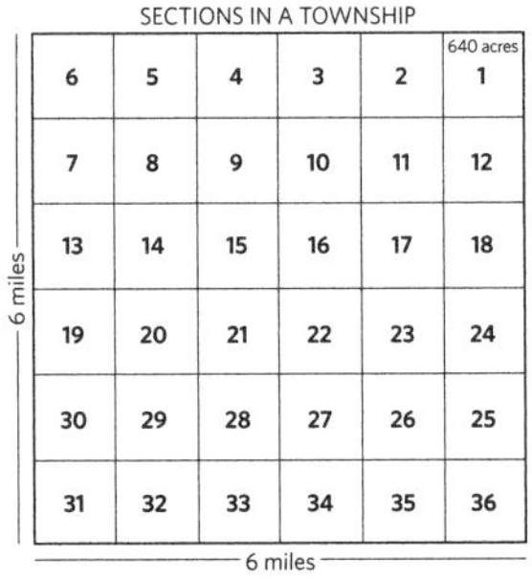

Public-land states divvied up parcels of property according to the rectangular survey system. The principal meridian—an imaginary north-south line—serves as the starting point for surveying a 24×24-mile tract. A tract is divided into 16 townships; every township (23,040 acres) contains 36 sections, each 1 square mile (640 acres).

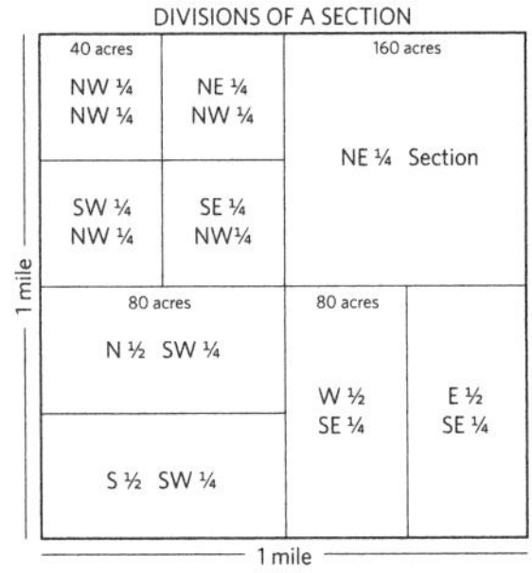

DIVISIONS OF A SECTION

40 acres		160 acres	
NW ¼ NW ¼	NE ¼ NW ¼	NE ¼ Section	
SW ¼ NW ¼	SE ¼ NW¼		
80 acres		80 acres	
N ½ SW ¼		W ½ SE ¼	E ½ SE ¼
S ½ SW ¼			

1 mile (vertical) — 1 mile (horizontal)

A section could be split into halves, quarters or otherwise. The descriptions of those subdivisions (such as "the north half of the southwest quarter," or N½ SW¼ for short) are called aliquot parts.

US TERRITORIAL ACQUISITION TIMELINE

1783 former British colonies

1803 Louisiana Purchase (828,800 square miles in what's now Arkansas, Missouri, Iowa, Oklahoma, Kansas, Nebraska, part of Minnesota, most of North Dakota and South Dakota, northeastern New Mexico, parts of Montana, Wyoming, and Colorado; and Louisiana west of the Mississippi River)

1819 Florida

1845 Texas

1846 Oregon Territory

1848 Mexican Cession (California, Nevada and Utah, plus parts of Colorado, New Mexico, Arizona and Wyoming)

1853 Gadsden Purchase (a strip of southern Arizona and New Mexico)

1867 Alaska, Midway Islands

1898 Hawaiian Islands, Philippine Islands, Guam, Puerto Rico

1899 American Samoa

1903 Panama Canal Zone

1917 Virgin Islands

MAJOR US POPULATION MIGRATIONS

LATE-1700S-1800S: As the United States grew, made treaties with Indians and awarded land bounties for Revolutionary War and War of 1812 service, settlers migrated from the original states to the Old Southwest (Alabama and Mississippi), the Old Northwest (Ohio, Indiana, Illinois, Michigan, Wisconsin and northeastern Minnesota), Kentucky and Tennessee.

1848-1855: The discovery of gold at Sutter's Mill in Coloma, Calif., touched off the California Gold Rush; an estimated 300,000 Americans and immigrants hurried to California.

1862-1934: The Homestead Act encouraged Americans to move to unoccupied land in the West. Eventually, 1.6 million homesteads were granted on 270,000,000 acres of federal land.

POST-RECONSTRUCTION: Racial oppression led many freedmen to leave the South. African-American migrants to Kansas in 1879 and 1880 became known as Exodusters.

LATE 1800s-EARLY 1900s: As the United States industrialized, towns and cities (mostly in the North) swelled with migrants from farms who went to work in mills, factories and offices.

1930-1940: By 1940, the severe dust storms of the Dust Bowl had caused 2.5 million people to flee the Plains states; 200,000 of them to California.

1910-1940: The Great Migration saw 1.75 million African-Americans leave the rural South for cities in the North and Midwest, such as New York, Baltimore, Philadelphia, Chicago, Detroit and St. Louis.

1940-1970: More than 5 million African-Americans moved from the South to cities in the North, Midwest and West.

GEOGRAPHY

MAJOR US MIGRATION ROUTES

BRADDOCK'S ROAD: New York and Pennsylvania
This route connected Cumberland, Md., on the Potomac River
to the Monongahela River south of present-day Pittsburgh. In
1813, construction began on the Cumberland Road (later, the
National Road), which followed much the same route.

CALIFORNIA TRAIL: Utah, California, Oregon, Washington
Blazed in 1841, this trail split off of the Oregon Trail at Soda
Springs, Idaho, after Fort Bridger. It followed the Bear River and
crossed the Great Salt Lake Desert and Sierra Nevadas.

CALIFORNIA GOLD RUSH MIGRANTS TRIED OTHER ROUTES:
Some went north of the Great Salt Lake and through a corner
of Idaho to rejoin the trail at the Humboldt River. From
Nevada, the Lassen Route aimed north of Sutter's Mill, while
the southerly Carson Route headed southwest.

CAROLINA ROAD: Virginia, the Carolinas and Georgia
An alternative to the Fall Line Road, the Carolina Road (also
called the Upper Road) tracked through Hillsboro and Char-
lotte, NC, in the 1750s. It originally extended to Greenville, SC,
but in 1828 connected to the Federal Road at Athens, Ga.

CHICAGO ROAD: Northwest Territory
This crude road from Detroit to Chicago, built between 1829
and 1836, brought pioneers to southern Michigan and Illinois.

DE ANZA TRAIL:
Arizona, Utah, California, Oregon, Washington
In 1776, Spanish Lt. Col. Juan Bautista de Anza led almost 300
people over 1,200 miles to settle Alta (Upper) California. The
first overland route connecting New Spain with San Francisco,
the US segment begins at Nogales, Ariz.

EL CAMINO REAL DE LOS TEJAS: Southwest
During the Spanish colonial period, this was the primary overland trail from what's now Mexico, across the Rio Grande to east Texas and the Red River Valley in what's now northwest Louisiana.

EL CAMINO REAL DE TIERRA ADENTRO: Southwest
This north-south route connected Mexico City with what's now northern New Mexico. Its US section stretches from El Paso, Texas, to San Juan Pueblo, NM.

FALL LINE ROAD: Virginia, the Carolinas and Georgia
Beginning in about 1735, travelers would leave King's Highway at Fredericksburg, Va., and head southwest to Augusta, Ga., at the head of the Savannah River. Eventually, many Alabama- and Mississippi-bound pioneers would follow the Fall Line Road to link up with the new Federal Road in Columbus, Ga.

FEDERAL ROAD: Alabama, Mississippi, Louisiana and Texas
In 1806 Congress appropriated $6,400 for this road to carry mail between Athens, Ga., and New Orleans. It was widened and partly rerouted in 1811; connecting Fort Stoddert, Ala. (north of Mobile), to Fort Wilkinson, Ga., on the Chattahoochee River, where the route merged with the original postal path.

GREAT VALLEY ROAD: Virginia, the Carolinas and Georgia
Known to Indians as the Great Warrior Path, this trail's forerunner reached from New York to present-day Salisbury, NC, where it connected with the Great Trading Path.

Its feeders included the Philadelphia Wagon Road, which in the 1740s, linked up with the Pioneer's Road from Alexandria, Va., and went on to Winchester, Va. The Great Valley Road also became a feeder into the Wilderness Road.

KING'S HIGHWAY: Virginia, the Carolinas and Georgia
Incorporating the Boston Post Road between Boston and New York, King's Highway could be called America's first interstate. It eventually stretched 1,300 miles south from Boston through most of the Colonies' important cities, to Charleston, SC.

MOHAWK TRAIL: New York and Pennsylvania
By 1770, this trail reached from Albany to Buffalo. The Catskill Turnpike overlapped it after the Revolutionary War. In 1825, the Erie Canal provided a waterway from Albany to Lake Erie.

MORMON TRAIL: Utah, California, Oregon, Washington
Mormon leader Brigham Young set off with his followers from Nauvoo, Ill., in 1846. They crossed Iowa and the Missouri River to the site of present-day Florence, Neb., then traced the north bank of the Platte River from Fort Kearny, Neb., to Fort Laramie, Wyo., where they turned southwest to Salt Lake City.

NATCHEZ TRACE: Tennessee, Mississippi, Louisiana
The first major north-south route in the South, the Natchez Trace followed Indian trails from Nashville, Tenn., to Natchez, Miss., on the Mississippi River. The 500-mile route was upgraded in 1806, and briefly supplanted by the Jackson Military Road, which reached New Orleans in 1820.

NATIONAL ROAD: Northwest Territory
Originally the Cumberland Road, the route was called the National Road by 1825 because of its Congressional funding. Construction of the 600-mile span, which eventually stretched from Cumberland, Md., (incorporating the old Braddock's Road) to Vandalia, Ill., began in 1811.

OLD SPANISH TRAIL: Southwest
This trail and its variants connected Santa Fe and Los Angeles, key outposts of what was then Mexico, from 1829 to 1848. The 2,700-mile trail crossed deserts, canyons and Death Valley.

OREGON TRAIL: Utah, California, Oregon, Washington
The Oregon Trail covered 2,000 miles in seven states. It stretched from Independence, Mo., to Fort Kearny, followed the south bank of the Platte River, crossed Wyoming to Fort Bridger and turned northwest through what's now Idaho. At The Dalles, Ore., migrants took the Columbia River or, after 1846, the safer but longer Barlow toll road across the Cascade Range to the Willamette Valley.

PENNSYLVANIA ROAD: New York and Pennsylvania
Incorporating the Great Conestoga Road and then later Lancaster Pike, the Pennsylvania Road connected Philadelphia to Pittsburgh. Much of the route west of Harrisburg followed the early path of Forbes Road.

RICHMOND ROAD: Kentucky and Tennessee
Many settlers bound for Kentucky traveled this route through Virginia from Richmond to Fort Chiswell, where it joined the Great Valley Road.

SANTA FE TRAIL: Southwest
More a commercial route than a migration path, this famous trail also was traveled by gold seekers and by American troops in the war with Mexico from 1821 until the railroad arrived in 1880. The 1,200-mile route crossed five states, from Franklin, Mo., to Santa Fe, NM.

STATE ROAD: Northwest Territory
Connecting to the Chicago Road, the State Road extended west from Chicago through Elgin and Rockford to Galena, Ill., on the Mississippi River.

WILDERNESS ROAD: Kentucky and Tennessee
Daniel Boone led six families through the Cumberland Gap into Kentucky in 1775, pathfinding what was originally called Boone's Trace but would become known as the Wilderness

Road when it was widened in 1796. Tennessee-bound settlers took the Knoxville Road south from Kentucky to the Nashville Road, or the Nickajack Trail from Fort Loudon (now in Tennessee) to the Chickasaw Trail (later renamed Robert's Road).

ZANE'S TRACE: Northwest Territory
In 1796 and 1797, Col. Ebenezer Zane built this road through Ohio between Wheeling, WV, and Maysville, Ky. The segment between Wheeling and Zanesville, Ohio, also called the Wheeling Road, was ultimately upgraded and incorporated into the National Road.

---

10 ONLINE MAPPING RESOURCES

BUREAU OF LAND MANAGEMENT GENERAL LAND OFFICE RECORDS <www.glorecords.blm.gov>
Besides federal land title records for Eastern public-land states, find the original surveyors' field notes, survey plats, master title plats, and images of land warrants issued as a reward for military service.

EHISTORY <ehistory.osu.edu>
With hundreds of searchable historical maps, this site is strongest on the Civil War.

GETTY THESAURUS OF GEOGRAPHIC NAMES ONLINE <www.getty.edu/research/conducting_research/vocabularies/tgn>
This database of more than 1.1 million locales includes current and historical spots around the world.

GOOGLE EARTH <arth.google.com>
"Fly" across the planet to view satellite imagery, maps, terrain, 3-D buildings and historical imagery.

HISTORIC MAP WORKS <www.proquest.com/en-US/catalogs/databases/detail/hmw.shtml>

ProQuest's collection (available through subscribing libraries) features more than 200,000 maps including property maps back to the late 1700s and antiquarian maps from the 15th to 19th centuries.

JEWISHGEN SHTETLSEEKER <www.jewishgen.org/communities>

Results in this database of localities in Central and Eastern Europe, the former Soviet Republics and Turkey link to historical names, maps and more.

LIBRARY OF CONGRESS AMERICAN MEMORY COLLECTION <memory.loc.gov>

Digitized maps here detail the Revolutionary Era, Louisiana Purchase, Civil War, World War II, railroads, US and Canadian cities and more.

ORDNANCE SURVEY: GET A MAP <www.ordnancesurvey.co.uk/oswebsite/getamap>

Search for small-scale, high-detail maps of anywhere in the United Kingdom, then print or copy to use on your genealogy website.

PERRY-CASTAÑEDA MAP COLLECTION <www.lib.utexas.edu/maps>

Find historical maps from around the world in this vast collection from the University of Texas library.

US GEOLOGICAL SURVEY <www.usgs.gov/pubprod>

Buy or download current maps, topographic maps back to 1882, and aerial maps. You also can look up places in the National Atlas or Geographic Names Information System.

SOCIAL
HISTORY

TIMELINE OF INVENTIONS

SOCIAL HISTORY

1596 Galileo invents the thermoscope.

1616 Castile soap is first made in Spain from olive oil.

1673 Johannes Hevelius builds a 140-foot-long refracting telescope.

1747 Andreas Marggraf extracts sugar from beets.

1765 Scotsman James Watt develops an improved version of Thomas Newcomen's steam engine.

1778 Scotsman Andrew Meikle invents the threshing machine.

1783 In France, the Marquis de Jouffray d'Abbans steams a small boat, the *Pyroscaphe*, across the Seine.

1784 A baker from Gouda makes the first Belgian waffle.

1793 Eli Whitney invents the cotton gin.

1796 Edward Jenner tests the first smallpox vaccine.

1807 First steamship, the *Clermont*, travels 150 miles from New York City to Albany in 32 hours.

1810 Vermont engraver James Wilson makes the first American globes for classroom use.

1819 France issues the first roller-skate patent.

1823 Samuel Read Hall receives a patent for a blackboard.

1838 British and American Steam Navigation Co.'s *Sirius* crosses the Atlantic entirely on steam power.

1843 First Christmas card designed by Englishman J.C. Horsley.

1844 Samuel Morse sends his first telegraph message.

1846 Belgian Adolphe Sax invents the saxophone.

1853 Potato chips are invented in Saratoga Springs, NY.

1857 Elisha Graves Otis installs the first commercial passenger elevator.

1858 The first working trans-Atlantic telegraph cable lasts only a month.

1858 Heinrich Geissler perfects the glass tube vacuum.

1866 Jack Daniel starts making whiskey in Lynchburg, Tenn.

1876 Edison patents the mimeograph.

1879 Constantin Fahlberg and Ira Remsen accidentally discover saccharin.

1882 Schuyler Skaats Wheele invents the electric fan.

1883 Jan E. Matzeliger patents a shoe-lasting machine that cuts the price of shoes in half.

1884 Lewis Waterman patents the first practical fountain pen.

1888 George Eastman sells cameras to amateurs with the slogan "You push the button, we do the rest."

1892 Lever voting machines first used in Lockport, NY.

1893 Charles and Frank Duryea convert a horse-drawn buggy to a gasoline-powered car.

1903 Orville and Wilbur Wright's Flyer sails 120 feet through the air in 12 seconds.

1904 D. McFarland Moore installs the first glowing-gas sign.

1907 Leo Baekeland creates Bakelite, the first completely synthetic manmade substance.

1908 Ford introduces the Model T; Melitta Benz invents the drip coffeemaker.

1907 The first photocopier, the rectigraph, is invented.

1910 Georges Claude displays the first neon light sign in Paris.

1933 The first drive-in movie theater opens in Camden, NJ.

1935 Beer is first sold in cans.

1938 Chester Carlson makes his first electrophotographic image (a precursor to the copy machine).

1938 Berlin, NH, native Earl Tupper invents Tupperware.

1945 First influenza vaccine released.

1956 First trans-Atlantic telephone cable is laid.

1959 Coors develops the aluminum beverage can.

TIMELINE OF DISASTERS

1747-1748 Record snowfalls in much of the United States.

1780 Hurricane hits in the Caribbean, destroying British and French fleets and killing an estimated 22,000.

1815 The Great September Gale is the first hurricane to strike New England in 180 years.

1816 Crops fail during a unseasonably cool summer in New England, called the "The Year Without a Summer," after ash from a volcanic eruption in Indonesia causes a worldwide climate shift.

1845 Rain in Ireland exacerbates the Great Potato Famine and encourages emigration.

1853 First major US rail disaster kills 46 at Norwalk, Conn.

1868-1869 Great Lakes storms sink or run aground more than 3,000 ships, killing 500-plus people

1869 108 die in a coal mine disaster in Avondale, Pa.

1871 Hundreds die in the Great Chicago Fire; other fires rage in Peshtigo, Wis., and Michigan.

1873 US Army Signal Corps issues its first hurricane warning.

1876 Train wreck near Ashtabula, Ohio, claims 83 lives.

1873-1877 Swarms of locusts damage $200 million in crops in Colorado, Minnesota, Nebraska, Wyoming and elsewhere.

1881 Hurricane hits Georgia and the Carolinas, killing 700.

1884 Feb. 19, tornadoes kill hundreds in Southeastern states.

1888 January blizzard kills hundreds in Montana, Dakota Territory and Nebraska; 400 die in the Northeast during the Great Blizzard.

1889 Heavy rains collapse a dam at Johnstown, Pa., killing more than 2,000.

1898 Avalanche near Sheep Camp, Alaska, is the deadliest event of the Klondike Gold Rush.

1900 Hurricane in Galveston, Texas, kills more than 6,000.

1906 Earthquake and ensuing fire kills hundreds in San Francisco.

1919 Great Boston Molasses Flood kills 21 and injures 150.

1925 Tornado kills nearly 700 in Illinois, Indiana and Missouri.

1927 Floods cause devastation and social upheaval along the Mississippi River.

1933-1939 Drought and overfarming in the Southern Plains create "Dust Bowl" storms; displaced farmers leave Oklahoma, Texas, Kansas and other states.

1937 Ohio River reaches record flood levels.

1938 Hurricane strikes New York and New England.

1944 Hartford, Conn., circus fire claims 168 lives

GLOSSARY OF ARCHAIC OCCUPATIONS

ACCOMPTANT: accountant

AERONAUT: balloonist or a trapeze artist

ALEWIFE: woman who keeps an alehouse or tavern

AMANUENSIS: secretary or stenographer

AXLE TREE MAKER: maker of axles for coaches and wagons

BAXTER: baker

BLUESTOCKING: female writer

BREWSTER: beer manufacturer

COHEN: priest

COOPER: barrel-maker

COLLIER: coal miner

COSTERMONGER: fruit seller

COURANTEER: journalist

CROCKER: potter

GAOLER: jailer

HIND: farm laborer

HUCKSTER: seller of small wares

HUSBANDMAN: tenant farmer

JOYNER/JOINER: skilled carpenter

LAVENDER: washer woman

LEECH/SAWBONES: washer woman

PEDASCULE: schoolmaster

PERAMBULATOR: surveyor

PERUKER: wigmaker

RATONER: rat catcher

SCAPPLER: person who roughly shapes stone in preparation for a mason

SCUTCHER: person who beats flax to soften the straw

SLOPSELLER: seller of ready-made clothes

SNOBSCAT: shoe repairer

TIDE WAITER: customs official

TIE MAKER: maker of wooden railway ties

TIPSTAFF: policeman

VULCAN: blacksmith

WEBSTER: weaver

WHITEWING: street sweeper

GLOSSARY OF ARCHAIC DISEASES

ABLEPSIA: blindness

ACUTE ANGINA: sore throat

APOPLEXY: paralyzed by stroke

BAD BLOOD, LUES DISEASE, FRENCH or **GREAT POX:** syphilis

BILIOUSNESS: jaundice caused by liver disease

BLACK DEATH, CAMP FEVER or **SHIP'S FEVER:** typhus

BRAIN FEVER: meningitis

CHILD BED FEVER: infection following childbirth

CHOLELITHIASIS: gall stones

CONGESTIVE FEVER or **CHILLS:** malaria

CONSUMPTION, AFRICAN CONSUMPTION, LUNG SICKNESS or **GALLOPING CONSUMPTION:** tuberculosis

CORYZA or **CATARRHAL:** cold or allergies

COSTIVENESS: constipation

CROUP: laryngitis, diphtheria or strep throat

DENGUE: infectious fever common in East Africa

DYSENTERY: diarrhea

DYSPEPSIA: heartburn, indigestion

FALLING SICKNESS or **CADUCEUS:** epilepsy

FATTY LIVER: cirrhosis

FEVER 'N AGUE: malarial fever

GREEN SICKNESS OR FEVER: anemia

GRIPPE, GRIP or **LAGRIPPE:** influenza (the flu)

INFANTILE PARALYSIS: polio

LUMBAGO: back pain

LUNG or **WINTER FEVER:** pneumonia

MORMAL: gangrene

NEURALGIA: general term for discomfort (e.g., "neuralgia in the head" is a headache)

PUERPERAL EXHAUSTION: death due to childbirth

PUTRID FEVER, CHIN COUGH, BLADDER IN THROAT, MALIGNANT SORE THROAT or **KRUCHHUSTEN:** diphtheria or whooping cough

QUINSEY: tonsillitis

SCREWS: rheumatism

SUGAR DIABETES: insulin-dependent diabetes

THRUSH or **APHTHA:** childhood disease; spots on mouth, lips and throat

TIMELINE OF US EPIDEMICS

1721 smallpox (New England)

1729 measles (Boston)

1738 smallpox (South Carolina)

1739-1740 measles (Boston)

1747 measles (Connecticut, New York, Pennsylvania, South Carolina)

1770s smallpox (Pacific Northwest)

1772 measles (North America)

1793-1798 yellow fever (recurs in Philadelphia)

1832 cholera (New York City, New Orleans and other major cities)

1837 smallpox (Great Plains)

1837 typhus (Philadelphia)

1841 yellow fever (Southern states)

1847 yellow fever (New Orleans)

1849 cholera (New York City; New Orleans, St. Louis and other cities along the Mississippi River)

1850 influenza (nationwide)

1851 cholera (Great Plains)

1852 yellow fever (nationwide, especially New Orleans)

1853 yellow fever (New Orleans)

1855 yellow fever (nationwide)

1860-1861: smallpox (Pennsylvania)

1862 smallpox (Pacific Northwest)

1865-1873 typhoid, yellow fever, scarlet fever (nationwide)

1865-1873 cholera (Baltimore, Memphis, Washington, DC)

1867 yellow fever (New Orleans)

1873-1875 influenza (nationwide)

1876 smallpox (South Dakota)

1878 yellow fever (lower Mississippi River valley)

1885 typhoid (Pennsylvania)

1886 yellow fever (Jacksonville, Fla.)

1900-1904 "Third Pandemic" (San Francisco)

1916 polio (nationwide)

1918 Spanish influenza (worldwide)

1949 polio (nationwide)

1952 polio (nationwide)

TYPICAL PRICES OF EVERYDAY ITEMS

1775 FLOUR: 15.36 shillings/hundredweight
    MOLASSES: 1.75 shillings/gallon
    SALT, COARSE: 2.13 shillings/bushel

1820 HARVARD TUITION: $300/year

1853 BEANS: 10.5 cents/quart
    BROWN SUGAR: 7.5-8 cents/pound
    FLOUR: 4-5 cents/pound
    PORK: 11 cents/pound
    SALT BEEF: 8.5-9 cents/pound

1863 EGGS: 25 cents/dozen
    HAIRCUT: 20 cents
    HOTEL STAY: $2.50 to $3 per night (New York)
    POTATOES: $6 (Southern United States)
    SUGAR: 12 to 15 cents/pound

1890s STEAMSHIP PASSAGE TO AMERICA: $25

1900 BREAD: 3 cents/loaf
    HOUSE: $4,000

1932 BREAD: 7 cents/loaf
    EGGS: 49 cents/dozen
    GAS: 18 cents/gallon
    HOUSE: $6,515
    MEN'S BROADCLOTH SHIRT: $1

1950 BREAD: 14 cents/loaf
    EGGS: 70 cents/dozen
    GAS: 27 cents/gallon
    HOUSE: $14,500

GREGORIAN CALENDAR
ADOPTION DATES BY COUNTRY

When the Gregorian calendar was introduced in 1582, it corrected math discrepancies in the old Julian calendar by dropping 10 days. That means you may need to adjust ancestors' birth and death dates that occurred before their countries adopted the new calendar.

ALASKA: Oct. 18, 1867

BRITISH EMPIRE (including the American colonies): Sept. 14, 1752

DENMARK (including Norway and some German states): March 1, 1700 (solar portion); 1776 (lunar portion)

DUTCH REPUBLIC
- **BRABANT**, **ZEELAND** and **STATEN-GENERAAL**: Dec. 25, 1582
- **GELDERLAND**: July 1700
- **OVERIJSSEL** and **UTRECHT**: December 1700
- **FRIESLAND** and **GRONINGEN:** January 1701

FRANCE: Dec. 20, 1582

GREECE: Feb. 15, 1923

HOLLAND: Jan. 12, 1583

ITALY (most): Oct. 15, 1582

POLISH-LITHUANIAN COMMONWEALTH: Oct. 15, 1582

PORTUGAL: Oct. 15, 1582*

PRUSSIA: Sept. 2, 1610

RUSSIA: Feb. 14, 1918

SOUTHERN NETHERLANDS (including what's now Belgium): Jan. 1, 1583

SWEDEN (included Finland): March 1, 1753

SPAIN: Oct. 15, 1582*

* Spanish and Portuguese colonies adopted the new calendar later than their mother countries because of slow communications.

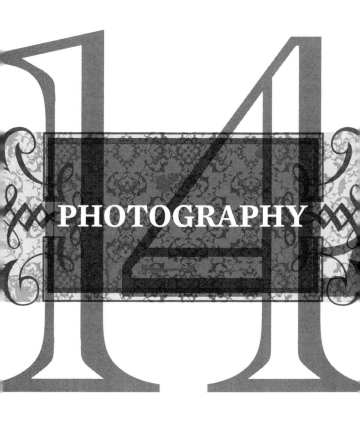

PHOTOGRAPHY

HISTORICAL PHOTO FORMATS

DAGUERREOTYPE: 1839-ABOUT 1865
A photo developed on a copper plate coated with highly polished silver, usually encased with a mat behind glass. You must hold the image at an angle to view it.

AMBROTYPE: 1852-ABOUT 1870
An image developed on glass backed with a dark varnish, cloth or paper. You can often see through the image where the backing has deteriorated.

TINTYPE: MID 1850s-PRESENT
Also known as a ferrotype or melainotype, the image was developed on a thin, blackened iron sheet coated with photo chemicals. The protective varnish may have darkened; the image also may rust.

CALOTYPE: 1841- ABOUT 1862
This early paper image, also called a talbotype, was common in England. The image may look fuzzy due to being printed with a paper negative. A salted paper print is a type of calotype with a clearer image. For both, the image appears to be embedded in the paper; a watermark may be visible.

ALBUMEN PRINT: 1850-EARLY 1900s
Developed from a glass negative on paper coated with egg whites and ammonium chloride, these images often were mounted onto thick paper to create 2.5x4-inch *cartes des visite*, and later, larger cabinet cards.

STEREOGRAPH: 1854-1938
Two nearly identical images mounted side by side resulted in a 3-D image when viewed through a stereoscope. A stereograph may be a daguerreotype or card photograph.

BLACK-AND-WHITE SNAPSHOTS: LATE 1880s-PRESENT
The first amateur cameras were pre-loaded with film; the operator returned the camera to the factory to obtain prints and more film. The small prints were mounted on cardstock in a variety of sizes.

POSTCARD: 1900-PRESENT
Photos developed on paper pre-printed with a postcard back could be mailed to family and friends.

AUTOCHROME: 1904-ABOUT 1937
These first commercially successful color pictures employed dyed vegetable starch to create color images on glass slides.

COLOR PAPER PRINTS: 1941-PRESENT
A negative image forms a positive color image when exposed onto photographic paper. Most are made from 35mm film.

POLAROID: 1947-PRESENT
A black-and-white or color image develops immediately after the film is exposed. Early on, the picture developed inside the camera and required a fixing agent. Later, the operator peeled away a backing to reveal the image; modern integral film enclosed photo chemicals inside a plastic packet.

6 PHOTO PRESERVATION TIPS

1. Don't stick anything to the surface of an image. Never laminate photos.

2. Never write on the front of a photo. Instead, write gently on the backs of old images with a soft lead pencil. For modern, plastic-coated papers, use a pen that's odorless when dry, waterproof, quick-drying and fade-resistant (available in craft- and art-supply stores).

3. Print digital images on photographic paper. If you print images at home, make them last as long as possible by using a good photo printer and photographic (not regular office paper).

4. Use good-quality storage materials. Keep old prints and cased images in acid-free, lignin-free boxes and envelopes. Albums also should be acid- and lignin-free; never the "magnetic" kind with adhesive pages. Mount photos with photo corners, not glue. Find supplies at photo and craft stores, and online retailers (run a web search on *archival storage*).

5. Store photos in a cool, dry, dark location. Exposure to high humidity, temperature extremes and light can cause discoloration and deterioration. Keep photos in a living area of your home, away from fireplaces and other heat sources. A shelf in an interior closet is ideal.

6. Scan and make copies of photos for display, rather than displaying the originals. Keep a high-resolution, TIFF-format preservation copy of each digitized photo, and make another copy for editing, viewing and sharing. Back up your digital images in multiple places.

6 PHOTO ID TIPS

1. Share the mystery photo with relatives (scan and e-mail, mail copies or visit). Ask what they know about who's in the photo, and when and where it was taken. Also ask whether they have similar photos.

2. Determine the format of the photo (daguerreotype? tintype? postcard?) to help you narrow the date is was taken. A stamp box on the back of a postcard can help you narrow the date even more.

3. Examine clothing, hairstyles and props in the photo, and consult a resource such as *Uncovering Your Ancestry Through Family Photographs* by Maureen A. Taylor (Family Tree Books) to learn when those styles were popular.

4. Study small background details by scanning the image at a high resolution (600 dpi or more) and enlarging it on your computer screen. You also can use a photographer's loupe to magnify details. Look for clues to the photo's location and the occasion.

5. Estimate the ages of people in the photo and compare the information to your genealogy research. For example, look for families in which the number, sex and ages of the children fit what you see in the photograph.

6. Are you trying to determine whether people in a group photo are related? Want to determine whether two photos show the same person? Examine facial features—especially the face shape, eyes, ears and nose—for similarities.

SOURCES OF FAMILY PHOTOGRAPHS

Missing some faces from your photo collection? One of these resources may have the image you seek:
- relatives
- family friends
- local historical society and library collections
- photo-reunion websites (such as DeadFred <deadfred.com> and AncientFaces <ancientfaces.com>)
- driver's and other licenses
- employment or military IDs
- newsletters for employers, clubs or fraternal organizations
- school yearbooks
- newspapers

- naturalization records
- immigrant identification cards
- passports
- criminal records
- mugbooks
- marriage certificates
- local and county histories
- published genealogies
- town and church centennial books
- biographical directories
- church membership directories
- eBay **<ebay.com>** and other auction websites

WRITING PHOTO CAPTIONS

When you caption your family photos—whether they're old black-and-white pictures or the snapshots you took just yesterday—include as much as you know of this information:

- full name(s) of the person or people pictured
- dates of birth and death of the person or people pictured
- name of the photographer
- date the photo was taken
- occasion or event shown
- place where the photo was taken
- provenance of the image: names of the original owner and those who've owned it since (or a source citation, if you found the image in a repository's collection or on a website)
- your name
- your relationship to the people pictured

PHOTO-EDITING TOOLS

Are you restoring digitized family photos? If your photo-editing software's autocorrect feature doesn't do the job, here's a rundown of the tools you may use:

AIRBRUSH: The airbrush tool simulates an actual airbrush or spray-paint can when applying a color. The longer you hold the airbrush over the image, the greater the effect. Airbrush options include the size and shape of the brush, as well as the spray's intensity.

BLUR: This tool softens portions of an image so they appear slightly out of focus, obscuring imperfections.

BURN: The burn tool is the opposite of Dodge: It darkens areas of the image that are too light.

CLONE (OR RUBBER STAMP): The clone tool does exactly what it implies: It replicates good areas of an image, so you can hide damaged areas. The source (the "good" area) can be from the same photo or an entirely different one.

DODGE: This lightens too-dark areas and brings out detail. Dodge takes its name from the traditional darkroom technique of holding back some of the light when printing a photo.

RED-EYE REDUCTION: This tool helps you get rid of the red-eye effect often caused by flash photography.

SMUDGE: Smudge softens an image by smearing details (rather than lightening the color, as the Blur tool does). Smudge is great for tackling tiny imperfections.

DIGITAL PHOTO RESOLUTION GUIDE

For best results when scanning your family photos, refer to this chart and set the resolution according to how you plan to use the digitized image.

INTENDED USE	RESOLUTION (DOTS PER INCH)	SIZE (IN PIXELS)	BEST FILE FORMAT
PHOTO PRINTS	300 dpi (Use a higher dpi if you plan to enlarge the photo)	1,200x1,800 (minimum)	JPG
POSTING ON WEBSITE	72 dpi	640x800	JPG
E-MAILING	72 dpi	640x800 (maximum, unless recipient plans to print)	JPG
ARCHIVING NEGATIVES OR SLIDES	Scan at highest optical resolution of the scanner (at least 1,200 dpi)	Varies, depending on size of original and scanner capability	TIFF or JPG
ARCHIVING PHOTOS	300 dpi	1,200 x 1,800 (minimum)	TIFF or JPG

MY FAVORITE REFERENCES

....

....

....

....

....

....

....

....

....

....

....

....

....

....

....

....

....

....

....

....

....

....

....

....

....

....

....

....

....

....

....

....

....

....

....

....

....

....

....

....

....

....

....

....

....

....

....

....

....

....

....

....

....

....

....

....

....

Acknowledgments

The content in this book was adapted from contributions by these *Family Tree Magazine* writers and genealogy experts.

Lisa A. Alzo

Sharon DeBartolo Carmack

Rick Crume

Nick D'Alto

Emily Anne Croom

David A. Fryxell

Lauren Gamber

Diane Haddad

Mark Haviland

Nancy Hendrickson

Sunny McClellan Morton

Dana Schmidt McCullough

Allison Stacy

Maureen A. Taylor

Index

Visit **<www.familytreemagazine.com>** for tips and tools to trace your ancestors. Sign up for our free e-mail newsletter and get a free digital issue of *Family Tree Magazine*!

family tree magazine